YESTERDAY'S VOICES: THE 12 UNIVERSAL LAWS
*A Prose and Poetry Anthology of
Inspiration and Reflection*

Other books compiled by
A. A. Willis

Yesterday's Voices on the Inner Life

Yesterday's Voices on the Inner Life, Volume Two

YESTERDAY'S VOICES: THE 12 UNIVERSAL LAWS

*A Prose and Poetry Anthology of
Inspiration and Reflection*

Compiled by A. A. Willis

Yesterday's Voices: The 12 Universal Laws
Copyright © 2023 by A. A. Willis

All rights reserved. This book or any portion thereof may not be reproduced or used in any manner whatsoever without the express written permission of the publisher, except for the use of brief quotations in a book review.

Printed in the United States of America

Luminare Press
442 Charnelton St.
Eugene, OR 97401
www.luminarepress.com

LCCN: 2023913836
ISBN: 979-8-88679-367-3

To all my spiritual sisters and brothers on life's journey

Table of Contents

Introduction 1
Prologue: The Universal Laws 7

1. The Law of Divine Oneness 19
2. The Law of Vibration 33
3. The Law of Correspondence 46
4. The Law of Attraction 66
5. The Law of Inspired Action 74
6. The Law of Perpetual Transmutation of Energy . . . 88
7. The Law of Cause and Effect 105
8. The Law of Compensation 118
9. The Law of Relativity 132
10. The Law of Polarity 151
11. The Law of Rhythm 171
12. The Law of Gender 182

Epilogue: The Universal Laws 196
References 198

INTRODUCTION

As Ralph Waldo Trine writes in his book, *In Tune with the Infinite*, "There is, then, this Spirit of Infinite Life and Power behind all which is the source of all. This Infinite Power is creating, working, ruling through the agency of great immutable laws and forces that run through all the universe, that surround us on every side. Every act of our every-day lives is governed by these same great laws and forces."

It has been inferred that the fundamental philosophical teachings on these laws and forces originated in ancient Egypt and ancient Greece, and have greatly influenced all the world religions, spiritual traditions, philosophers, and classical poets for thousands of years.

Yesterday's Voices: The 12 Universal Laws is the third book in the series of *Yesterday's Voices* inspirational anthologies. It is a compilation of verse and prose selections from historical sources that refer to, and exemplify, the timeless and immutable laws that govern the universe and our human experience. These timeless laws and forces have been recognized by, and referenced in writings by prophets, philosophers, sages, poets, theologians, mystics, and scientists throughout history. Literature over the ages has variously described them as "The 12 Universal Laws", "The 12 Spiritual Laws", "Laws of the Universe", "Laws of the

Spirit", "Laws of Nature", "Universal Principles", "Cosmic Principles", or "Ordinances or Laws of Heaven." They have been called laws, principles, timeless truths, guidelines for living, and more. The number and descriptive name may vary depending on the school of thought and the age in question. Whether expressed in the writings of the world religions, ancient and modern philosophy, spirituality, Perennial Philosophy, New Thought, New Age, or the classic literature of the ancient world, these timeless principles continue to supply wisdom and guidance for our current times.

The literature selections collected here highlight and celebrate the benefits of living in harmony with these laws and principles, no matter their number or their collective name. A compelling and intriguing feature is the broad spectrum of inspirational and didactic literature from the past - be it scripture, epic, essay, novel, treatise, sermon, play, poem, or prayer – that refers to these timeless laws of unity, oneness, change, and interconnections in all their manifestations, either directly or indirectly. The extremely abundant and diverse references to these laws and principles in sacred literature, and in the many writings of well-known and lesser-known sages, thinkers, and poets throughout history, all combine to validate their significance and merit in our human experience.

In essence, all the 12 laws are intertwined in a wide-ranging variety of ways, and can be thought of as 12 arcs of the same circle, each with a slightly different focus, but still interconnected and unified as part of the same whole. As it relates to our human condition, the Law of Attraction is based on thinking and mental states, and therefore has interdependence with the Laws of Vibration, Inspired Action, Correspondence, Cause and Effect, Compensation, Gender. The Law of Polarity, based on its attribute of complementary opposites, has interdependence with the Laws of Cause and Effect, Gender, Relativity. All the laws have qualities and associations such as these, and this helps reinforce the concept of unity in our Universe.

The principle of dualism, the two-sided nature of things, is one of the key aspects shared by and linking all the Universal Laws. A common coin, for purposes of analogy to the individual Universal Laws, has two opposing and complementary sides, a "head" and a "tail", and essentially could not exist as it does if the two sides were not interconnected and interdependent. This dualism is an omnipresent principle in our world, observed within all the Universal Laws. Even in the concepts of oneness and unity the principle of duality is found, as exemplified in the complementary opposites of unity and diversity. Collectively, all of the other universal laws have this feature in some form or fashion:

- In the Law of Vibration: motion and rest.
- In the Law of Correspondence: "as within, so without," "as above, so below."
- In the Law of Attraction: attraction and repulsion.
- In the Law of Inspired Action: action and results.
- In the Law of Perpetual Transformation of Energy: change from one form or state to another.
- In the Law of Cause and Effect: cause and effect, or action and reaction.
- In the Law of Compensation: what we give and what we receive.

- In the Law of Relativity: beneficial or unbeneficial perspectives on circumstances and experiences.
- In the Law of Polarity: complementary opposites.
- In the Law of Rhythm: periodic or regulated cycles between opposing elements or states of existence.
- In the Law of Gender: balance between the two poles of energy, masculine and feminine; balance between "Masculine Principles" and "Feminine Principles."

Throughout literature, phenomena and principles of nature are compared to the human condition via analogy, metaphor, and simile. Aspects of nature have been commonly used as a metaphor for our human life and experience in all genres of writing. Literature describing the universal laws has routinely referenced the natural world in comparing how these laws manifest in our lives. And just as there is a two-sided nature to each of the universal laws, these literary devices have a two-sided aspect in comparing one thing to another, in these cases the outer natural world and our inner human condition or experience. These comparative narrative techniques have been used extensively by writers of all types and in all ages, especially the poets and naturalists. Our human condition is as much a part of the natural world as a tree, a bird, a cloud, energy waves, or a thunderstorm, and is subject to the same laws and forces. It is evident in so much of the prose and poetry from the past that these comparisons are key in fully describing and referring to these timeless laws and how they relate to our human experience.

This collection includes a wide array of eclectic selections from prose and poetry of the past. The selections included here mention or give examples of these universal laws and forces, either directly or sometimes in muted and understated fashion. The use of a large diversity of sources helps demonstrate the broad scope and range of references to the universal laws that occurs in yesterday's literature from many genres, and how these laws and forces manifest in the world and govern all aspects of our lives. Included at the beginning of each set of selections on the individual Universal Laws is a brief summary of some key aspects of each law as gleaned from literature sources.

This anthology is a consequence of a long-time interest in collecting inspirational and thought-provoking literature on the inner life from the voices of yesterday. This particular volume was inspired by the many categories of literature that were found to give examples of these eternal Universal Laws. The selections and arrangements presented here are based on personal perspectives on these items. Another individual might select and arrange things a bit differently depending on their outlook. Conceding the limitless scope of this subject, it is hoped that this collection, even in a very small way, might help illustrate how valuable these laws and principles can be if embraced by the individual. In letting the voices of yesterday speak directly, unfiltered, to the reader, perhaps this collection, or particular selections, will bring some degree of inspiration, enlightenment, and pleasure to those who reflect on the manifold aspects of our human condition as we navigate along our journey through life.

—A. A. Willis
2023

Prologue

The Universal Laws

The Universal Laws apply to tangible and intangible things in the Universe. Their claim is that, by aligning with these laws, an individual can manifest order in their life and live more successfully in the world. These principles can be found in some form in the sacred literature of all the world religions. It is claimed that these laws exist and manifest themselves in the world whether one accepts them or not.

The Universal Laws recognize the three planes of our reality as the physical, the mental, and the spiritual. The principle of oneness and unity in life maintains that these planes are all interconnected, and when they are in harmony, we have our fullest, most satisfying life. When these planes are out of harmony, we experience many of the problems and difficulties in life.

Philosophical, scientific, and spiritual literature sources declare the following about the Universal Laws: they regulate creation and describe the realities of the universe, matter, energy, and our inner being; they govern and define our inner and outer worlds; they are essential for aligning one's self to the nature, harmony, and spirit of the universe; and they are useful as aids for the formation of character, and in order to live one's best life.

There is a divine sequence running throughout the universe. Within and above and below the human will incessantly works the Divine will. To come into harmony with it and thereby with all the higher laws and forces, to come then into league and to work in conjunction with them, in order that they can work in league and in conjunction with us, is to come into the chain of this wonderful sequence. This is the secret of all success. This is to come into the possession of unknown riches, into the realization of undreamed-of powers.

—Ralph Waldo Trine
In Tune with the Infinite.

Before beginning, and without an end,
    As space eternal and as surety sure,
Is fixed a Power divine which moves to good,
    Only its laws endure.

It maketh and unmaketh, mending all;
    What it hath wrought is better than hath been;
Slow grows the splendid pattern that it plans
    Its wistful hands between.

This is its work upon the things ye see,
    The unseen things are more; men's hearts and minds,
The thoughts of peoples and their ways and wills,
    Those, too, the great Law binds.

—Edwin Arnold
The Light of Asia: Or, The Great Renunciation.

Nature acts by general laws; that is, the occurrences of the world in which we find ourselves, result from causes which operate according to fixed and constant rules.

When we speak of material nature as being governed by laws, it is sufficiently evident that we use the term in a manner somewhat metaphorical. The laws to which man's attention is primarily directed are moral laws; rules laid down for his actions; rules for the conscious actions of a person; rules which, as a matter of possibility, he may obey or may transgress; the latter event being combined, not with an impossibility, but with a penalty. But the Laws of Nature are something different from this; they are rules for that which things are to do and suffer; and this by no consciousness or will of theirs. They are rules describing the mode in which things do act; they are invariably obeyed; their transgression is not punished, it is excluded. The language of a moral law is, man shall not kill; the language of a Law of Nature is, a stone will fall to the earth.

These two kinds of laws direct the actions of persons and of things, by the sort of control of which persons and things are respectively susceptible; so that the metaphor is very simple; but it is proper for us to recollect that it is a metaphor, in order that we may clearly apprehend what is implied in speaking of the Laws of Nature.

—WILLIAM WHEWELL
"Treatise III." *The Bridgewater Treatises.*

After every foolish day we sleep off the fumes and furies of its hours; and though we are always engaged with particulars, and often enslaved to them, we bring with us to every experiment the innate universal laws. These, while they exist in the mind as ideas, stand around us in nature forever embodied, a present sanity to expose and cure the insanity of men.

—Ralph Waldo Emerson
Nature.

The position we have been led to take up is not that the Spiritual Laws are analogous to the Natural Laws, but that they are the same Laws. It is not a question of analogy but of Identity.

The Natural Laws, as the Law of Continuity might well warn us, do not stop with the visible and then give place to a new set of Laws bearing a strong similitude to them. The Laws of the invisible are the same Laws, projections of the natural not supernatural. Analogous Phenomena are not the fruit of parallel Laws, but of the same Laws—Laws which at one end, as it were, may be dealing with Matter, at the other end with Spirit.

—Henry Drummond
"Introduction." *Natural Law in the Spiritual World.*

It has been just said, that there is no branch of human work whose constant laws have not close analogy with those which govern every other mode of man's exertion. But, more than this, exactly as we reduce to greater simplicity and surety any one group of these practical laws, we shall find them passing the mere condition of connection or analogy, and becoming the actual expression of some ultimate nerve or fibre of the mighty laws which govern the moral world.

—John Ruskin
"Introductory." *The Seven Lamps of Architecture.*

We find ourselves suddenly living and moving in the midst of the universe, — as a part of it, and not as its aim and object. We find ourselves living, not under capricious and arbitrary conditions, unconnected with the constitution and movements of the whole, but under great, general, invariable laws, which operate on us as a part of the whole.

—Harriet Martineau
"Preface." *The Positive Philosophy of Auguste Comte.*

In the universe, all is done according to law, by the regular and orderly action of the forces thereof; there is a constant mode of operation, which never changes. Nothing is done by human magic, nothing by divine miracle.

—Theodore Parker
Lessons from the World of Matter and the World of Man.

On the whole, as this wondrous planet, Earth, is journeying with its fellows through infinite Space, so are the wondrous destinies embarked on it journeying through infinite Time, under a higher guidance than ours.

—Thomas Carlyle
"Signs of the Time."

We are slow to wake up to a sense of the divinity that hedges us about. The great office of science has been to show us this universe as much more wonderful and divine than we have been wont to believe; shot through and through with celestial laws and forces; matter, indeed, but matter informed with spirit and intelligence; the creative energy inherent and active in the ground underfoot not less than in the stars and nebulae overhead.

—John Burroughs
"The Phantoms Behind Us." *Time and Change.*

As timber is carried away by the stream to places high and low, so even is the body led by Law to whatever awaits it at its proper time.

—*Vivekachudamani*
"Liberation." *The Spirit of the Upanishads; Or, The Aphorisms of the Wise.*

It is said in the Book of Poetry, "The ordinances of Heaven, how profound are they and unceasing!"

—*The Doctrine of the Mean.* (Confucianism).

Remember, man, "the Universal Cause
Acts not by partial, but by general laws;"
And makes what happiness we justly call
Subsist not in the good of one, but all.
There's not a blessing individuals find,
But some way leans and hearkens to the kind.

—Alexander Pope
An Essay on Man. Moral Essays and Satires.

Man……— He is the work of nature.— He exists in Nature.—He is submitted to the laws of Nature.—He cannot deliver himself from them:—cannot step beyond them even in thought…

Therefore……. let him study this Nature, learn her laws, contemplate her energies, observe the immutable rules by which she acts.— Let him apply these discoveries to his own felicity, and submit in silence to her precepts,

Let him yield to the decrees of a universal power, which can never be brought within his comprehension, nor ever emancipate him from those laws imposed on him by his essence.

Experience teaches that Nature acts by simple, regular, and invariable laws. It is by his senses, man is bound to this universal Nature; it is by his perception he must penetrate her secrets; it is from his senses he must draw experience of her laws.

—Baron d'Holbach (Paul-Henri Thiry)
"Nature and her Laws." *The System of Nature, Or, Laws of the Moral and Physical World.*

There is, then, this Spirit of Infinite Life and Power behind all which is the source of all. This Infinite Power is creating, working, ruling through the agency of great immutable laws and forces that run through all the universe, that surround us on every side. Every act of our every-day lives is governed by these same great laws and forces. Every flower that blooms by the wayside, springs up, grows, blooms, fades, according to certain great immutable laws. Every snowflake that plays between earth and heaven, forms, falls, melts, according to certain great unchangeable laws.

—Ralph Waldo Trine
In Tune with the Infinite.

How the might of Nature sways
All the world in ordered ways,
How resistless laws control
Each least portion of the whole.

—Boethius
"Song II, Book III." *The Consolation of Philosophy of Boethius.*

I cannot open my eyes without admiring the art that shines throughout all nature; the least cast suffices to make me perceive the Hand that makes everything. Nay, what is called the art of men is but a faint imitation of the great art called the laws of Nature, and which the impious did not blush to call blind chance.

—Francois de Salignac de La Mothe-Fénelon
A Demonstration of the Existence and Attributes of God.

The life, the fortune, and the happiness of every one of us, and, more or less, of those who are connected with us, do depend upon our knowing something of the rules of a game infinitely more difficult and complicated than chess. It is a game which has been played for untold ages, every man and woman of us being one of the two players in a game of his or her own. The chessboard is the world, the pieces are the phenomena of the universe, the rules of the game are what we call the laws of Nature. The player on the other side is hidden from us. We know that his play is always fair, just and patient. But also we know, to our cost, that he never overlooks a mistake, or makes the smallest allowance for ignorance.

—Thomas Henry Huxley
"LXXXIII." *Aphorisms and Reflections.*

I dreamed a dream last night, when all was still,
When earth in sleep forgot her murmurings;
I saw the soul, the spirit—what you will—
Of this vast world; I saw the heart of things.

I saw that back of everything there lies
This wondrous, shining essence, finer far
Than all the gathered gold of western skies
More lasting still than suns or planets are.

This, this is real, for this it is that gives
Life, color, motion, form, to what we see.
This hidden something that forever lives,
Sustaining all with subtle certainty.

In vain do men of science seek to prove
The hidden world that throbs behind the seen;
The ever-present Cause of things that move,
Eludes their searching sight, however keen.

As well might sunbeams seek to prove the sun
And rivulets the ocean, as that man—
A living flame from out the Central One—
Should seek to prove the Source where life began.

Would man but grasp, with focused powers of mind
The subtle laws that rule the finer realm,
Abandoning the lesser aims that blind,
The grosser joys that dull and overwhelm,

This dawning century would bring to light
The deepest truths for which we vainly grope;
Would open up new worlds to human sight,
In large fulfilment of our highest hope!

—Angela Morgan.
"Reality." *Utterance And Other Poems.*

For to each thing God hath given
Its appointed time;
No perplexing change permits He
In His plan sublime.

—Boethius
"Song VI, Book I." *The Consolation
of Philosophy of Boethius.*

HARMONY is the universal law of Nature. Of all the numberless forms of animals and plants that deck the surface of the globe, there is not one that is not perfectly fitted for its peculiar sphere. The configuration of our earth, and the physical laws that govern the waters and the atmosphere, are in complete unison with the wants of organic life; and suns and planets wander harmoniously through illimitable space. And as it now is, thus it ever has been; for the annals of our globe bear witness, throughout all the changes of the primeval world, to the concord which has constantly reigned between the physical condition of the earth and its inhabitants at each successive epoch.

In the following pages I have endeavoured to point out some of the most striking examples of this fundamental truth, which so forcibly proclaims the unity of creation.

—Georg Hartwig
"Preface." *The Harmonies of Nature or
The Unity of Creation.*

Myself am a little universe. Let my passions be moderate and my likes and dislikes be well-regulated, and then my conduct will conform of itself to the laws of the universe, in which the elements are so harmoniously combined. Heaven and earth are the great parents of all creation.

—Hung Ying-Ming
Musings of a Chinese Vegetarian.

Chapter 1

The Law of Divine Oneness

The Law of Divine Oneness highlights the interconnectedness of all things, both physical and non-physical, and emphasizes that there is a unity that permeates the universe in all things, both seen and unseen.

This basic unity underlies the diversity in our world, whether that diversity exists in aspects of the natural world, in the varying moods of our consciousness, or in the spiritual and religious traditions that have emerged throughout human history.

As one aspect of the spiritual perspective of this law of oneness, the Perennial Philosophy is a viewpoint that teaches the unity of all religions and that the same ultimate Truth is present in a variety of forms in all the religious traditions.

All are but parts of one stupendous whole,
Whose body Nature is, and God the soul;
That, changed through all, and yet in all the same;
Great in the earth, as in the ethereal frame;
Warms in the sun, refreshes in the breeze,
Glows in the stars, and blossoms in the trees,
Lives through all life, extends through all extent,
Spreads undivided, operates unspent;

Breathes in our soul, informs our mortal part,
As full, as perfect, in a hair as heart:
As full, as perfect, in vile man that mourns,
As the rapt seraph that adores and burns:
To him no high, no low, no great, no small;
He fills, he bounds, connects, and equals all.

—Alexander Pope
An Essay on Man. Moral Essays and Satires.

Whether we read the *Upanishads*, the *Bhagavad Gita*, or the *New Testament*, we find ourselves in exactly the same atmosphere as regards the meaning and nature of the spiritual life: it is that which knows the oneness, that in which unity is complete.

—Annie Besant
The Meaning and Method of the Spiritual Life.

Turn, turn, my wheel! The human race,
Of every tongue, of every place,
Caucasian, Coptic, or Malay,
All that inhabit this great earth,
Whatever be their rank or worth,
Are kindred and allied by birth,
And made of the same clay.

—Henry Wadsworth Longfellow
"Keramos." Keramos and Other Poems.

There is one animal, one plant, one matter and one force. The laws of light and of heat translate each other; — so do the laws of sound and of colour; and so galvanism, electricity and magnetism are varied forms of the selfsame energy. While the student ponders this immense unity, he observes that all things in Nature, the animals, the mountain, the river, the seasons, wood, iron, stone, vapor, have a mysterious relation to his thoughts and his life; their growths, decays, quality and use so curiously resemble himself, in parts and in wholes, that he is compelled to speak by means of them. His words and his thoughts are framed by their help. Every noun is an image. Nature gives him, sometimes in a flattered likeness, sometimes in caricature, a copy of every humor and shade in his character and mind. The world is an immense picture-book of every passage in human life.

—RALPH WALDO EMERSON
"Poetry and Imagination." *Letters and Social Aims. Volume 8.*

Things are not run by blind chance—there is Law under everything. Everything has some connection with every other thing—every person has a relationship with every other person. All is One—the manifestations are varied, but there is but One reality. There is a great plan underlying all Life, and Life itself is in accordance with that plan. Nothing ever happens. Every occurrence has a bearing on every other occurrence. Chance has no part in the plan—everything is in accord with well-ordered laws. There is always an end in view in every thought, word or act. We are constantly being used for the benefit of the whole. There is no escape—and when we get to know we cease to wish to escape. He who understands not Law is constantly struggling, striving, fighting, and contending against it, and, producing friction, he feels pain. He who understands something of Law ceases to contend against it—he lets it work through him, and is carried along with a mighty force, doing each day the best he knows how, expressing himself in the best possible manner, sailing to the right and to the left, with the wind and against the wind, but still being borne on by the mighty current and resisting it not. He enjoys every mile of the journey, seeing new sights and hearing new sounds—moving on ever. He who understands not, rebels at being swept along—he wishes to stay where he is, but there is no such thing as staying—life is motion—life is growth.

—WILLIAM WALKER ATKINSON
Nuggets of the New Thought.

To regard the soul and body as one, or to ascribe to consciousness a physiological origin, is not detracting from its divinity, it is rather conferring divinity upon the body. One thing is inevitably linked with another – the higher forms with the lower forms, the butterfly with the grub, the flower with the root, the food we eat with the thought we think, the poem we write, or the picture we paint, with the processes of digestion and nutrition. How science has enlarged and ennobled and purified our conception of the universe; how it has cleaned out the evil spirits that have so long terrified mankind, and justified the verdict of the Creator: "and behold it was good"! With its indestructibility of matter, its conservation of energy, its inviolability of cause and effect, its unity of force and elements throughout sidereal space, it has prepared the way for a conception of man, his origin, his development, and in a measure his destiny, that at last makes him at home in the universe.

—John Burroughs
"The Divine Soil." *Leaf and Tendril.*

Things great and small,
We are but parts of the Eternal All;
We live not in a barren, baseless dream;
No endless, ineffectual chain
Of chance successions launched in vain;
But every beat of Time,
Each sun that shines or fails to shine,
Each animate life that comes to throb or cease,
Each life of herb or tree
Which springs aloft and then has ceased to be,
Each change of strife and peace,
Each soaring thought sublime,
Each deed of wrong and blood,
Each impulse towards an unattained good, —
All with a sure, unfaltering working tend
To one Ineffable, Beatific End.

—Lewis Morris
"The Ode of Change." *The Ode of Life.*

How present and sensible to my inner sense is the unity of everything! It seems to me that I am able to pierce to the sublime motive which, in all the infinite spheres of existence, and through all the modes of space and time, every created form reproduces and sings within the bond of an eternal harmony.

—Henri-Frédéric Amiel
Amiel's Journal. The Journal Intime of Henri-Frédéric Amiel.

The trouble is that in the end we shall be driven to admit the unity of the universe so completely as to be compelled to deny that there is either an external or an internal, but must see everything both as external and internal at one and the same time, subject and object—external and internal—being unified as much as everything else.

—Samuel Butler
The Way of All Flesh.

A purpose, an intention, a design is evident in everything; and when our comprehension is so far enlarged as to contemplate the first rise of this visible system, we must adopt, with the strongest conviction, the idea of some intelligent cause, or author. The uniform maxims too, which prevail throughout the whole frame of the universe, naturally, if not necessarily, lead us to conceive this intelligence as single and undivided, where the prejudices of education oppose not so reasonable a theory. Even the contrarieties of nature, by discovering themselves every where, become proofs of some consistent plan, and establish one single purpose or intention, however inexplicable and incomprehensible.

—David Hume
Essays Moral, Political, and Literary.

Science tends more and more to reveal to us the unity that underlies the diversity of nature. We must have diversity in our practical lives; we must seize Nature by many handles. But our intellectual lives demand unity, demand simplicity amid all this complexity. Our religious lives demand the same. Amid all the diversity of creeds and sects we are coming more and more to see that religion is one, that verbal differences and ceremonies are unimportant, and that the fundamental agreements are alone significant.

—John Burroughs
"The Natural Providence." *Accepting the Universe. Essays in Naturalism.*

There is one Great Law which exacts unconditional obedience, one unifying principle which is the basis of all diversity, one eternal Truth wherein all the problems of earth pass away like shadows. To realize this Law, this Unity, this Truth, is to enter into the Infinite, is to become one with the Eternal.

—James Allen
The Way of Peace.

When we know that living things are formed of the same elements as the inorganic world, that they act and react upon it, bound by a thousand ties of natural piety, is it probable, nay is it possible, that they, and they alone, should have no order in their seeming disorder, no unity in their seeming multiplicity, should suffer no explanation by the discovery of some central and sublime law of mutual connection?

—Thomas Henry Huxley
"LIII." *Aphorisms and Reflections.*

Look round our world; behold the chain of love
Combining all below and all above.
See plastic Nature working to this end,
The single atoms each to other tend,
Attract, attracted to, the next in place
Formed and impelled its neighbour to embrace.
See matter next, with various life endued,
Press to one centre still, the general good.
See dying vegetables life sustain,
See life dissolving vegetate again:
All forms that perish other forms supply
(By turns we catch the vital breath, and die),
Like bubbles on the sea of matter borne,
They rise, they break, and to that sea return.
Nothing is foreign: parts relate to whole;
One all-extending, all-preserving soul
Connects each being, greatest with the least;
Made beast in aid of man, and man of beast;

All served, all serving: nothing stands alone;
The chain holds on, and where it ends, unknown.

—Alexander Pope
An Essay on Man. Moral Essays and Satires.

Society alone represents a more or less complete unity. The individual must content himself with being a stone in the building, a wheel in the immense machine, a word in the poem. He is a part of the family, of the state, of humanity, of all the special fragments formed by human interests, beliefs, aspirations, and labors. The loftiest souls are those who are conscious of the universal symphony, and who give their full and willing collaboration to this vast and complicated concert which we call civilization.

—Henri-Frédéric Amiel
Amiel's Journal: The Journal Intime
of Henri-Frédéric Amiel.

The masters of old attained unity with the Tao.
Heaven attained unity and became pure.
The earth attained unity and found peace.
The spirits attained unity so they could minister.
The valleys attained unity that they might be full.
Humanity attained unity that they might flourish.
Their leaders attained unity that they might set the example.
This is the power of unity.

—Lao-Tzu
Tao Te Ching.

In the course of this progress each man learns by sad and bitter experience the intangible unity of all beings, finding that nothing that injures one can be good for any, that that which brings happiness to all can alone bring happiness to each. Not the happiness of the greater number but the happiness of all is necessary for the happiness of one.

Oneship is not in the lower but in the higher, not in the body or the mind but in the spirit, the divine, the eternal life. Virtue and happiness are ultimately the same, because virtue is that which serves the life of all, not the separated life, and it is virtue merely because it aids evolution and is lifting the many towards the One.

—Annie Besant
"Problems of Ethics." *Some Problems of Life.*

"Tis easy, as Experience may aver,
To pass from general to particular.
But most laborious to direct the soul
From studying parts, to reason on the whole:
Thoughts, train'd on narrow subjects, to let fall;
And learn the unison of each with all.

—Elizabeth Barrett Browning
"An Essay on Mind." *An Essay on Mind, with Other Poems.*

There is a close analogy between the world of nature and the world of spirit. They bear the impress of the same hand; and hence the principles of nature and its laws are the types and shadows of the Invisible. Just as two books, though on different subjects, proceeding from the same pen, manifest indications of the thought of one mind, so the worlds, visible and invisible, are two books written by the same finger, and governed by the same idea. Or rather, they are but one book, separated into two only by the narrow range of our ken. For it is impossible to study the universe at all without perceiving that it is one system. Begin with what science you will, as soon as you get beyond the rudiments, you are constrained to associate it with another.

—Frederick William Robertson
"First Series. Sermon 14."
Sermons Preached at Brighton.

These facts have always suggested to man the sublime creed, that the world is not the product of manifold power, but of one will, of one mind; and that one mind is everywhere active, in each ray of the star, in each wavelet of the pool; and whatever opposes that will, is everywhere balked and baffled, because things are made so, and not otherwise. Good is positive. Evil is merely privative, not absolute: it is like cold, which is the privation of heat. All evil is so much death or nonentity. Benevolence is absolute and real. So much benevolence as a man hath, so much life hath he. For all things proceed out of this same spirit, which is differently named love, justice, temperance, in its different applications, just as the ocean receives different names on the several shores which it washes. All things proceed out of the same spirit, and all things conspire with it.

—Ralph Waldo Emerson
The Divinity School Address.

There is a deeper fact in the soul than compensation, to wit, its own nature. The soul is not a compensation, but a life. The soul *is*. Under all this running sea of circumstance, whose waters ebb and flow with perfect balance, lies the aboriginal abyss of real Being. Essence, or God, is not a relation, or a part, but the whole. Being is the vast affirmative, excluding negation, self-balanced, and swallowing up all relations, parts, and times within itself. Nature, truth, virtue, are the influx from thence. Vice is the absence or departure of the same.

—Ralph Waldo Emerson
"Compensation." *Essays, First Series.*

The fact that there is a spiritual power in us, that is to say, a power which testifies to the unity of our life with the life of others, which impels us to regard others as other selves—this fact comes home to us even more forcibly in sorrow than in joy.

—Felix Adler
Life and Destiny: Or, Thoughts from the Ethical Lectures of Felix Adler.

O, woven in one wide Loom thro' the throbbing weft of the whole,
One in spirit and flesh, one in body and soul,
Tho' the leaf were alone in its falling, the bird in its hour to die,
The heart in its muffled anguish, the sea in its mournful cry,

One with the flower of a day, one with the withered moon
One with the granite mountains that melt into the noon
One with the dream that triumphs beyond the light of the spheres,
We come from the Loom of the Weaver that weaves the Web of Years.

—A<small>LFRED</small> N<small>OYES</small>
"The Loom of Years."

Constantly regard the universe as one living being, having one substance and one soul; and observe how all things have reference to one perception, the perception of this one living being; and how all things act with one movement; and how all things are the co-operating causes of all things which exist; observe too the continuous spinning of the thread and the contexture of the web.

—M<small>ARCUS</small> A<small>URELIUS</small>
The Meditations of Marcus Aurelius.

Whoever, at the coarsest sound,
Still listens for the finest,
Shall hear the noisy world go round
To music the divinest.

Whoever yearns to see aright
Because his heart is tender,
Shall catch a glimpse of heavenly light
In every earthly splendor.

The Law of Divine Oneness

So, since the universe began,
And till it shall be ended,
The soul of Nature, soul of Man,
And soul of God are blended!

—Theodore Tilton
"The Mystery Of Nature." *The Sexton's Tale,*
and Other Poems.

Chapter 2

The Law of Vibration

The Law of Vibration asserts that everything - every atom, object, and living thing - is some form of energy and is in constant motion, vibrating, and never rests. This law is entwined with the Law of Attraction ("like attracts like"), the Law of Rhythm ("cycles"), and the Law of Transmutation of Energy ("change").

It applies to the subatomic world and the world of galaxies, and all the worlds between. Related terms and concepts describing this universal vibration are motion, pulsations, and musical references. Some philosophical and spiritual schools of thought apply this Law of Vibration to intangible things, such as thoughts, feelings, beliefs, and ideas as well as to tangible physical objects.

The musical references and comparisons in literature that allude to the Law of Vibration, directly or indirectly, use "sound", "harmony", "resonance", or "rhythm" as related terms and concepts in illustrating its manifestation in the universe and as an essential element in Creation. Throughout history musical comparisons have been an integral component in writings on religion, philosophy, human nature, and the natural world.

"Nothing rests; everything moves; everything vibrates."

— *The Kybalion.*

The great Third Hermetic Principle—the Principle of Vibration—embodies the truth that Motion is manifest in everything in the Universe—that nothing is at rest—that everything moves, vibrates, and circles.

Modern Science has proven that all that we call Matter and Energy are but "modes of vibratory motion,".....

But the Hermetic Teachings go much further than do those of modern science. They teach that all manifestation of thought, emotion, reason, will or desire, or any mental state or condition, are accompanied by vibrations, ...

—"Vibration." *The Kybalion.*

Observation and reflection ought to convince us, that every thing in Nature is in continual motion—that there is not a single part, however small, that enjoys repose—that Nature acts in all—that she would cease to be Nature if she did not act. Practical knowledge teaches us, that without unceasing motion, nothing could be preserved—nothing could be produced—nothing could act in this Nature. Thus the idea of Nature necessarily includes that of motion. But it will be asked, and not a little triumphantly, from whence did she derive her motion?

We say this motion is a manner of existence, that flows, necessarily, out of the nature of matter; that matter moves by its own peculiar energies; that its motion is to be attributed to the force which is inherent in itself....

—Baron d'Holbach (Paul-Henri Thiry)
"Of Motion, and its Origin." *The System of Nature, Or, Laws of the Moral and Physical World.*

The sound of summer is everywhere—in the passing breeze, in the hedge, in the broad-branching trees, in the grass as it swings; all the myriad particles that together make the summer are in motion. The sap moves in the trees, the pollen is pushed out from grass and flower, and yet again these acres and acres of leaves and square miles of grass blades—for they would cover acres and square miles if reckoned edge to edge—are drawing their strength from the atmosphere. Exceedingly minute as these vibrations must be, their numbers perhaps may give them a volume almost reaching in the aggregate to the power of the ear. Besides the quivering leaf, the swinging grass, the fluttering bird's wing, and the thousand oval membranes which innumerable insects whirl about, a faint resonance seems to come from the very earth itself. The fervour of the sunbeams descending in a tidal flood rings on the strung harp of earth. It is this exquisite undertone, heard and yet unheard, which brings the mind into sweet accordance with the wonderful instrument of nature.

—Richard Jefferies
The Pageant of Summer.

The human mind is Nature's keyboard, on which her harmonies and discords are sounded by the touch of invisible fingers.

—James Lendall Basford
Sparks from the Philosopher's Stone.

We know now, that words and thoughts are a tremendous vibratory force, ever moulding man's body and affairs.

— Florence S. Shinn
The Game of Life and How to Play It.

Our work is double. The pendulum of our life swings ever backward and forward, with its double beat,— time, eternity,— eternity, time. But the word time is what we hear, and that side of the perpendicular is the side of the vibration we see and know. But all things we do are provisional, only our character is ultimate and final.

—Theodore Parker
Lessons from the World of Matter and the World of Man.

But while change is the law, certain great ideas flow fresh through the ages, and control us effectually as in the days of Pericles. Mankind, it has been said, is always advancing, man is always the same. The love, hope, fear and faith that make humanity, and the elemental passions of the human heart, remain unchanged, and the secret of inspiration in any literature is the capacity to touch the cord that vibrates in a sympathy that knows nor time nor place.

—William Osler
A Way of Life.

For prayer will in time make the human countenance its own divinest altar; years upon years of true thoughts, like ceaseless music shut up within, will vibrate along the nerves of expression until the lines of the living instrument are drawn into correspondence, and the harmony of visible form matches the unheard harmonies of the mind.

—James Lane Allen
The Choir Invisible.

Consider and act with reverence to the true ends of existence. This world is but the vestibule of an immortal life. Every action of your life touches on some chord that will vibrate in eternity; these thoughts and motives within you stir the pulses of a deathless spirit.

—Edwin Hubbel Chapin
"Advice to the Young."

That boy, in doing that right act, struck a cord that extends through the whole universe, touches all moral intelligence, visits every world, vibrates along its whole extent, and conveys its vibrations to the very bosom of God.

—Thomas Binney
Is it Possible to Make the Best of Both Worlds?

Trust thyself: every heart vibrates to that iron string.

—Ralph Waldo Emerson
"Self-Reliance." *Essays, First Series.*

Let us understand from this standpoint how the brain has to be changed, how it has to be refined; and how it has to be improved, how all its connecting links have to be fashioned and manufactured for the purposes of the expression of the Higher Consciousness……….. Do not suppose that whilst your passions are still ruling you, whilst their demands can upset the mind, whilst the body is unrestrained, you are ready to receive on the mind the reflection of the Self. You must learn to rule the body, to keep it under control, by giving it proper sleep, and proper exercise, and proper food, satisfying all its needs, so as to keep it in health, not as a master, but as the obedient servant of consciousness. Hear what Shri Krishna says: "Verily Yoga is not for him who eateth too much, nor who abstaineth to excess, nor who is addicted to too much sleep, nor even to wakefulness, O Arjuna."* [* *Bhagavad Gita*, vi 16.]

There is to be no extreme on either side; no torturing of the body that is to be the instrument, but also no yielding to the body that it may imagine itself the master of the Self. Where this training is followed, the brain becomes able to receive the subtler vibrations, without loss of equilibrium, and health is not sacrificed to gain delicacy and sensitiveness. The yogi is most exquisitely sensitive, but perfectly sane.

Having controlled and purified the body, we can make it sensitive to the higher vibrations, responsive to the sounding of the sublimer notes. But to do this, we must lose our interest in the lower, and become indifferent to the attractions of the outer life. Vairagya, dispassion, we must have, for that is a condition of the Higher Consciousness revealing itself in the lower world.

—Annie Besant
"The Larger Consciousness." *The Laws of the Higher Life*.

In the final analysis, all things in Nature, from a fleeting thought or emotion to the hardest piece of diamond or platinum, are modes of motion or vibration.

—Charles F. Haanel
"Medicine." *Mental Chemistry*.

The everyday cares and duties, which men call drudgery, are the weights and counterpoises of the clock of time, giving its pendulum a true vibration and its hands a regular motion….

—Henry Wadsworth Longfellow
Kavanagh: A Tale.

The Father spake! In grand reverberations
Through space rolled on the mighty music-tide,
While to its low, majestic modulations,
The clouds of chaos slowly swept aside
Nor yet has ceased that sound—his love revealing
Though, in response, a universe moves by!
Throughout eternity, its echo pealing—
World after world awakes in glad reply!
And wheresoever, in his rich creation,
Sweet music breathes—in wave, or bird, or soul—
'Tis but the faint and far reverberation
Of that great tune to which the planets roll!

—Frances S. Osgood
"Music." *The Female Poets of America.*

Nature is an aeolian harp, a musical instrument whose tones are the re-echo of higher strings within us.

— Novalis.
(Georg Philipp Friedrich Freiherr von Hardenberg).

Then, while the mighty mists were still concealing
The sphereless world (not yet an asteroid),
God ordered heavenly music to go pealing
Through all the silence of the earthly void.

Within a shining cloud, that veiled their faces,
Ten thousand seraphs, each with harp in hand,

Flew chanting through the still and empty spaces
That afterward were filled with sea and land.

The stars, that on the morning of creation
Together sang to Him who made them fair,
First caught their canticle of adoration
From this immortal murmur in the air.

Before the mountains had their high upheaval,
Before the caverns of the deep were laid,
This was creations harmony primeval,
The rhythm to which the whirling world was made.

Th' Almighty, who decreed this Chant Celestial,
By its primordial melody designed
To chord to it all cadences terrestrial,
As this was chorded to th' Eternal Mind

But discord on the earth is ever raging,
For human hate is quenchless in its flame,
Yet, high above the wars that men are waging,
The angels still go singing, all the same.

Above the bedlam world, but never near it,
Their floating chant is caroled through the sky,
So faint and far that mortals hardly hear it,
Yet he who hearkens hears it by and by.

It smites the ear with such a soft vibration
That some who hear it think it not a sound,
But fancy it their spirit's own pulsation,
That thrills the sense with ecstasy profound.

It chimes to deserts and dim wildernesses,
In swift pursuit where wandering feet have trod;

And whom it overtakes, it sweetly blesses, -
And fills the pilgrim with the peace of God.

> —Theodore Tilton
> "The Chant Celestial." *Thou and I: a lyric of human life. With other poems.*

Is it any weakness, pray, to be wrought on by exquisite music? to feel its wondrous harmonies searching the subtlest windings of your soul, the delicate fibres of life where no memory can penetrate, and binding together your whole being, past and present, in one unspeakable vibration....

> —George Eliot (Mary Ann Evans)
> *Adam Bede.*

While the optic nerve holds up to us the magic mirror in which Nature appears in all her beauty, the auditive nerve opens to our perception the wondrous realms of sound. The undulating atmospherical vibrations produced by the voices of a choral band, or by the instruments of an orchestra, strike its delicate membranes and awaken musical sensations, which, transmitted to the soul, attune it to joy or to sorrow, rouse it to martial ardour, or exalt it to feelings of the deepest piety.

> —Georg Hartwig
> "Chapter XXVIII. Man." *The Harmonies of Nature or The Unity of Creation.*

The waves upon water are always objects of pleasing interest. From the ripples of the pond to the billows of the ocean, their beauty and their sublimity are sources of perennial inspiration to the poet and the painter. But there is an invisible realm of air-waves of a far subtler and more wonderful order. The water-waves belong to the sensuous eye and to art, but the aerial pulsations belong to the eye of the imagination and to science, the great revelator of the super-sensuous harmonies of the universe. Water-waves afford an agreeable spectacle, and have little further concern for us; but the waves of air take hold of our highest life, for the multitudinous sounds of Nature by which we are soothed and exhilarated, all the delights of music, the pleasures of speech, and the sweet experiences of social intercourse, are made possible only through their agency. Besides, air-waves form one link in the chain of agencies by which we pass from the material to the spiritual world. The first is the capacity by which matter may be thrown into vibration; second, the properties of air by which it can take up the impulses of vibration in the form of waves; third, those properties of the mechanism of hearing by which it can take up the motion of air-pulses; and, fourth, those properties of nerves by which they can take up the tympanic vibrations and translate them into feeling or consciousness.

—"Wave-Action in Nature."
Popular Science Monthly. Volume 3, May 1873.

Sometimes, on Sundays, I heard the bells, the Lincoln, Acton, Bedford, or Concord bell, when the wind was favorable, a faint, sweet, and, as it were, natural melody, worth importing into the wilderness. At a sufficient distance over the woods this sound acquires a certain vibratory hum, as if the pine needles in the horizon were the strings of a harp which it swept. All sound heard at the greatest possible distance produces one and the same effect, a vibration of the universal lyre, just as the intervening atmosphere makes a distant ridge of earth interesting to our eyes by the azure tint it imparts to it. There came to me in this case a melody which the air had strained, and which had conversed with every leaf and needle of the wood, that portion of the sound which the elements had taken up and modulated and echoed from vale to vale. The echo is, to some extent, an original sound, and therein is the magic and charm of it. It is not merely a repetition of what was worth repeating in the bell, but partly the voice of the wood....

—Henry David Thoreau
"Sounds." *Walden.*

As there are but few souls that know how far the harmony of outward nature with our own reaches, and in how very great a degree the whole creation is but an Aeolian harp, with longer and shorter strings, with slower and swifter vibrations, passive before a divine breath.

—Jean Paul Friedrich Richter
Hesperus or Forty-Five Dog-Post-Days Vol. I. A Biography.

All is in vibration. From the tiniest atom to the greatest sun, everything is in a state of vibration. There is nothing in absolute rest in nature. A single atom deprived of vibration would wreck the universe. In incessant vibration the universal work is performed. Matter is being constantly played upon by energy and countless forms and numberless varieties result, and yet even the forms and varieties are not permanent. They begin to change the moment they are created, and from them are born innumerable forms, which in turn change, and give rise to newer forms, and so on and on, in infinite succession. Nothing is permanent in the world of forms, and yet the great Reality is unchangeable. Forms are but appearances—they come, they go, but the Reality is eternal and unchangeable.

—Yogi Ramacharaka
Hatha Yoga.

Chapter 3

The Law of Correspondence

The Law of Correspondence states that there is always a correspondence between the outer physical world and the inner mental world of the individual – "as within, so without".

The Spiritual Law of Correspondence is an esoteric principle of ancient theology derived from the teachings of Hermetic philosophy, the perennial philosophy, and other early religious systems. According to this principle, there is resonance between our inner and outer worlds. This principle declares an actual existent relationship between the outer world of matter and experience, and our inner world of mind. Quieting the mind through reflection, meditation, and being in nature are actions that are said to help this correspondence in positive directions.

This law maintains that how we see our outer environment, relationships, circumstances, and life experiences corresponds to and reflects the states of our inner life. To change and improve our outer world experiences and circumstances, we first must change our inner world of thoughts, attitudes, and beliefs.

And conversely, the observation and experience of the outer natural world has the power to influence our interior world through realization of our unity and connection with all life. As such, this law has interdependence with the laws of "Oneness", "Polarity", and the other universal laws. Throughout recorded history, sacred literature and many celebrated philosophers, poets, and spiritual teachers have proclaimed the parallels between the human spirit and other aspects of the natural world. An individual's inner thoughts and values, and how they relate to the outer world, combine to define one's character and outlook on life.

"As above, so below; as below, so above."

This Principle embodies the truth that there is always a Correspondence between the laws and phenomena of the various planes of Being and Life.

This Principle is of universal application and manifestation, on the various planes of the material, mental, and spiritual universe—it is a Universal Law.

—"The Seven Hermetic Principles."
The Kybalion.

Every thing the individual sees without him corresponds to his states of mind, and every thing is in turn intelligible to him, as his onward thinking leads him into the truth to which that fact or series belongs.

—Ralph Waldo Emerson
"History." *Essays, First Series.*

That the beauty which looks from the whole face of Nature, and is interwoven with every fibre of it, is not the less, because it requires a living soul for its existence, as real a truth as the gravitation of the earth's particles or the composition of its materials,—that careful noting and familiar knowledge of this beauty reveals a new aspect of the world, which will amply repay the observer,—and that the Poets are, in a special way, kindlers of sensibility, teachers who make us observe more carefully, and feel more keenly the wonders that are around us.

—John Campbell Shairp
"Preface." *On Poetic Interpretation of Nature.*

It is, indeed, but a feeble expression of the truth to say that the infinities revealed to us by Science, –the infinitely great in the one direction, and the infinitely small in the other, –go far beyond anything which had occurred to the unaided imagination of Man, and are not only a never-failing source of pleasure and interest, but seem to lift us out of the petty troubles and sorrows of life.

—Sir John Lubbock
"The Beauties of Nature."
The Pleasures of Life: Part II.

As with events, so is it with thoughts. When I watch that flowing river, which, out of regions I see not, pours for a season its streams into me, I see that I am a pensioner; not a cause, but a surprised spectator of this ethereal water; that I desire and look up and put myself in the attitude of reception, but from some alien energy the visions come.

—Ralph Waldo Emerson
"The Over-Soul." *Essays, First Series.*

Nature is full of form and movement. No steadfast gaze into any landscape can go unrewarded. The life of the soul is linked to that of nature, both by love and by knowledge, and through centuries of habit, the exquisite images of earth, air, and sea, have been loved and responded to in literature as a means presenting force, modulated and attempered into style.

—Orison Swett Marden
The Consolidated Library, Volume 8.

All life is from within out. This is something that cannot be reiterated too often. The springs of life are all from within. This being true, it would be well for us to give more time to the inner life than we are accustomed to give to it, especially in this Western world.

There is nothing that will bring us such abundant returns as to take a little time in the quiet each day of our lives.

—Ralph Waldo Trine
Character- Building Thought Power.

Then he returned to the window, and saw that the sun had gone quite down behind the window. And there came on the twilight of an August evening. And his soul grew calm with it; and it felt religious to him. And he said to himself, "Never, never do great thoughts come to a man while he is discontented or fretful. There must be quiet in the temple of his soul, before the windows of it will open for him to see out of them into the infinite. Quiet is what heavenly powers move in. It is in silence the stars move on; and it is in quiet our souls are visited from on high."

—WILLIAM MOUNTFORD
Thorpe: A Quiet English Town, and Human Life Therein.

You never enjoy the world aright, till the Sea itself floweth in your veins, till you are clothed with the heavens, and crowned with the stars: and perceive yourself to be the sole heir of the whole world, and more than so, because men are in it who are every one sole heirs as well as you. Till you can sing and rejoice and delight in God, as misers do in gold, and Kings in sceptres, you never enjoy the world.

Till your spirit filleth the whole world, and the stars are your jewels; till you are as familiar with the ways of God in all Ages as with your walk and table: till you are intimately acquainted with that shady nothing out of which the world was made: till you love men so as to desire their happiness, with a thirst equal to the zeal of your own: till you delight in God for being good to all: you never enjoy the world.

—THOMAS TRAHERNE
Centuries of Meditations.

While to the poet and the thoughtful man the changes of times and seasons are in the highest degree beautiful and suggestive, even to the most indifferent and selfish they are surrounded with an agreeable interest. None view their progress without regard, however little they may be attracted by their sweet pictures and phenomena, or moved by the amenities and wisdom of their ministry. This is because the changes incidental to nature are, on the one hand, a kind of counterpart or image of the occurrences and vicissitudes of human life…

—Leo Hartley Grindon
"Time and Seasons." *Life: Its Nature, Varieties, and Phenomena.*

That prayer or inner communion with the spirit thereof—be that spirit 'God' or 'law'—is a process wherein work is really done, and spiritual energy flows in and produces effects, psychological or material, within the phenomenal world.

—William James
The Varieties of Religious Experience.

Intellectual achievements are the result of thought consecrated to the search for knowledge, or for the beautiful and true in life and nature.

Spiritual achievements are the consummation of holy aspirations. He who lives constantly in the conception of noble and lofty thoughts, who dwells upon all that is pure and unselfish, will, as surely as the sun reaches its zenith and the moon its full, become wise and noble in character, and rise into a position of influence and blessedness.

Achievement, of whatever kind, is the crown of effort, the diadem of thought.

—James Allen
As a Man Thinketh.

Mind is the Master power that molds and makes,
And Man is Mind, and ever more he takes
The Tool of Thought, and shaping what he wills,
Brings forth a thousand joys, a thousand ills—
He thinks in secret and it comes to pass;
Environment is but his looking-glass.

—James Allen
As A Man Thinketh.

Everything that we call Invention or Discovery in the higher sense of the word is the serious exercise and activity of an original feeling for truth, which, after a long course of silent cultivation, suddenly flashes out into fruitful knowledge. It is a revelation working from within on the outer world, and lets a man feel that he is made in the image of God. It is a synthesis of World and Mind, giving the most blessed assurance of the eternal harmony of things.

—Johann Wolfgang Von Goethe
"Science." *The Maxims and Reflections of Goethe.*

We have always need of the infinite, the eternal, the absolute; and since science contents itself with what is relative, it necessarily leaves a void, which it is good for man to fill with contemplation, worship, and adoration. "Religion," said Bacon, "is the spice which is meant to keep life from corruption," and this is especially true to-day of religion taken in the Platonist and oriental sense. A capacity for self-recollection— for withdrawal from the outward to the inward—is in fact the condition of all noble and useful activity.

—Henri-Frédéric Amiel
Amiel's Journal: The Journal Intime of Henri-Frédéric Amiel.

Our circumstances and environment are formed by our thoughts. We have, perhaps, been creating these conditions unconsciously. If they are unsatisfactory the remedy is to consciously alter our mental attitude and see our circumstances adjust themselves to the new mental condition. There is nothing strange or supernatural about this. It is simply the Law of Being. The thoughts which take root in the mind will certainly produce fruit after their kind. The greatest schemer cannot "gather grapes of thorns, or figs of thistles." To improve our conditions we must first improve ourselves. Our thoughts and desires will be the first to show improvement.

—Charles F. Haanel
"Vibration." *Mental Chemistry.*

The law of correspondences between spiritual and material things is wonderfully exact in its workings. People ruled by the mood of gloom attract to them gloomy things. People always discouraged and despondent do not succeed in anything, and live only by burdening some one else. The hopeful, confident, and cheerful attract the elements of success. A man's front or back yard will advertise that man's ruling mood in the way it is kept. A woman at home shows her state of mind in her dress. A slattern advertises the ruling mood of hopelessness, carelessness, and lack of system. Rags, tatters, and dirt are always in the mind before being on the body. The thought that is most put out brings its corresponding visible element to crystallize about you as surely and literally as the visible bit of copper in solution attracts to it the invisible copper in that solution. A mind always hopeful, confident, courageous, and determined on its set purpose, and keeping itself to that purpose, attracts to itself out of the elements things and powers favorable to that purpose.

—Prentice Mulford
Your Forces, and How to Use Them, Volume 1.

One ship drives east and another drives west
With the self-same winds that blow;
'Tis the set of the sails
And not the gales
That tells them the way to go.
Like the winds of the sea are the winds of fate
As we voyage along through life;
'Tis the set of the soul
That decides its goal
And not the calm or the strife.

—Ella Wheeler Wilcox
"The Winds of Fate." *Poems of Optimism.*

Which of us feels, or knows, that he wants peace?

There are two ways of getting it, if you do want it. The first is wholly in your own power; to make yourselves nests of pleasant thoughts. Those are nests on the sea indeed, but safe beyond all others; only they need much art in the building. None of us yet know, for none of us have been taught in early youth, what fairy palaces we may build of beautiful thought—proof against all adversity. Bright fancies, satisfied memories, noble histories, faithful sayings, treasure-houses of precious and restful thoughts, which care cannot disturb, nor pain make gloomy, nor poverty take away from us—houses built without hands, for our souls to live in.

—John Ruskin
"The Eagle's Nest." *The Works of John Ruskin.*

There is one animal, one plant, one matter and one force. The laws of light and of heat translate each other; — so do the laws of sound and of colour; and so galvanism, electricity and magnetism are varied forms of the selfsame energy. While the student ponders this immense unity, he observes that all things in Nature, the animals, the mountain, the river, the seasons, wood, iron, stone, vapor, have a mysterious relation to his thoughts and his life; their growths, decays, quality and use so curiously resemble himself, in parts and in wholes, that he is compelled to speak by means of them. His words and his thoughts are framed by their help. Every noun is an image. Nature gives him, sometimes in a flattered likeness, sometimes in caricature, a copy of every humor and shade in his character and mind. The world is an immense picture-book of every passage in human life. Every object he beholds is the mask of a man.

> "The privates of man's heart
> They speken and sound in his ear
> As tho' they loud winds were";

for the universe is full of their echoes.

Every correspondence we observe in mind and matter suggests a substance older and deeper than either of these old nobilities.

—RALPH WALDO EMERSON
"Poetry and Imagination." *Letters and Social Aims. Volume 8.*

All that we are is the result of what we have thought: it is founded on our thoughts, it is made up of our thoughts. If a man speaks or acts with an evil thought, pain follows him, as the wheel follows the foot of the ox that draws the carriage.

All that we are is the result of what we have thought: it is founded on our thoughts, it is made up of our thoughts. If a man speaks or acts with a pure thought, happiness follows him, like a shadow that never leaves him.

—*THE DHAMMAPADA.*

At the same time, life will always be to a large extent what we ourselves make it. Each mind makes its own little world. The cheerful mind makes it pleasant, and the discontented mind makes it miserable. "My mind to me a kingdom is," applies alike to the peasant as to the monarch. The one may be in his heart a king, as the other may be a slave. Life is for the most part but the mirror of our own individual selves. Our mind gives to all situations, to all fortunes, high or low, their real characters. To the good, the world is good; to the bad, it is bad. If our views of life be elevated—if we regard it as a sphere of useful effort, of high living and high thinking, of working for others' good as well as our own—it will be joyful, hopeful, and blessed. If, on the contrary, we regard it merely as affording opportunities for self-seeking, pleasure, and aggrandisement, it will be full of toil, anxiety, and disappointment.

—SAMUEL SMILES
"Chapter XII. The Discipline of Experience."
Character.

Better is it when the stream of outward and inner life are both full and broad—when the glories of the material universe attract the gaze, the realm of literature and learning invite the willing feet to wander in paths where poetry has planted many flowers, philosophy many a sturdy oak of truth, which centuries cannot overthrow—and when, on the other hand, men do not forget to retire often within, and find their own minds kingdoms, where many a noble thought spontaneously grows; their own souls heavens, where, the busy world withdrawn, they commune much with their own aspirations, fight many a noble battle with whatever hinders their spiritual peace.

—ARTHUR BUCKMINSTER FULLER
"Preface." *Life Without and Life Within, Or, Reviews, Narratives, Essays, and Poems,* by Margaret Fuller.

There is a Power, whose care
Teaches thy way along that pathless coast,—
The desert and illimitable air
Lone wandering, but not lost.
All day thy wings have fanned,
At that far height, the cold thin atmosphere;
Yet stoop not, weary, to the welcome land,
Though the dark night is near.
And soon that toil shall end,
Soon shalt thou find a summer home, and rest,
And scream among thy fellows; reeds shall bend,
Soon, o'er thy sheltered nest.
Thou'rt gone, the abyss of heaven
Hath swallowed up thy form, yet, on my heart
Deeply hath sunk the lesson thou hast given,
And shall not soon depart.
He, who, from zone to zone,
Guides through the boundless sky thy certain flight,
In the long way that I must trace alone,
Will lead my steps aright.

—WILLIAM CULLEN BRYANT
"To a Waterfowl."

How countless and how multiform the scenes
Nature presents, expanding as we tread
Her sacred precincts! With what various tongues
She teaches, and how vast the wisdom gained!
Nature is man's best teacher. She unfolds
Her treasures to his search, unseals his eye,
Illumes his mind, and purifies his heart.

An influence breathes from all the sights and sounds
Of her existence; she is Wisdom's self.
Rest yields she to the "weary" of the earth—
Its "heavy-laden" she endows with strength.

—Alfred Billings Street
"Nature." *The Poems of Alfred B. Street.*

The human mind, actively occupied, is apt to go astray. When we sit down quietly, with no idea to agitate the mind, we can commune with nature. If we see a cloud appearing on the horizon, we shall follow it in its wandering in the blue. If we hear rain dripping from the eaves, we shall feel our bosoms cooled and purified. If we listen to birds singing, we shall be cheered up by their songs. If we see flowers falling, we shall know that anything flourishing cannot last long. Thus, when we are in communion with nature, what spot or what object is there that does not teach us something about the truth?

—Hung Ying-Ming
Musings of a Chinese Vegetarian.

Every flower that gives its fragrance to the wandering air, leaves its influence on the soul of man. The wheel and swoop of the winged creatures of the air suggest the flowing lines of subtle art. The roar and murmur of the restless sea, the cataract's solemn chant, the thunder's voice, the happy babble of the brook, the whispering leaves, the thrilling notes of mating birds, the sighing winds, taught man to pour his heart in song, and gave a voice to grief and hope, to love and death.

—Robert Green Ingersoll
"Nature." *The Philosophy of Ingersoll.*

For I have learned
To look on nature, not as in the hour
Of thoughtless youth, but hearing oftentimes
The still, sad music of humanity,
Nor harsh nor grating, though of ample power
To chasten and subdue. And I have felt
A presence that disturbs me with the joy
Of elevated thoughts; a sense sublime
Of something far more deeply interfused,
Whose dwelling is the light of setting suns,
And the round ocean, and the living air,
And the blue sky, and in the mind of man,
A motion and a spirit, that impels
All thinking things, all objects of all thought,
And rolls through all things. Therefore am I still
A lover of the meadows and the woods,
And mountains; and of all that we behold
From this green earth; of all the mighty world
Of eye and ear, both what they half-create,

And what perceive; well pleased to recognize
In nature and the language of the sense,
The anchor of my purest thoughts, the nurse,
The guide, the guardian of my heart, and soul
Of all my moral being.

—William Wordsworth
"Lines Written a Few Miles Above Tintern Abbey."
Lyrical Ballads, with a Few Other Poems.

The fundamental fact in our metaphysic constitution is the correspondence of man to the world, so that every change in that writes a record in the mind. The mind yields sympathetically to the tendencies or law which stream through things, and make the order of nature; and in the perfection of this correspondence or expressiveness, the health and force of man consist. If we follow this hint into our intellectual education, we shall find that it is not propositions, not new dogmas and a logical exposition of the world, that are our first need; but to watch and tenderly cherish the intellectual and moral sensibilities, those fountains of right thought, and woo them to stay and make their home with us. Whilst they abide with us, we shall not think amiss.

—Ralph Waldo Emerson
"Success." *Society and Solitude.*

Cherish your visions. Cherish your ideals. Cherish the music that stirs in your heart, the beauty that forms in your mind, the loveliness that drapes your purest thoughts, for out of them will grow all delightful conditions, all heavenly environment; of these, if you but remain true to them, your world will at last be built.

—James Allen
As a Man Thinketh.

The dawn is filled with earth's awakenings, —
A river's song along the ferned ravine,
The humming of an insect host unseen,
The whir and whistle of invisible wings.

A mood of melody pervades all things;
The very clouds have music in their mien,
And I can almost believe I hear the green
Grass breathe beneath my light heart while it sings.

Ah! unto those who love her Nature shows
Domains she grants not to indifferent eyes,
Vast realms that make kings' crowns seem dowerless;

Here leaps the quickened thought, — the dwarfed soul grows,
Each sense unto some higher sense replies, —
Yet this is what men say is idleness

—Mary Ashley Townsend
"LX." *Distaff and Spindle: Sonnets.*

If thou art worn and hard beset
With sorrows, that thou wouldst forget,
If thou wouldst read a lesson, that will keep
Thy heart from fainting and thy soul from sleep,
Go to the woods and hills! No tears
Dim the sweet look that Nature wears.

— Henry Wadsworth Longfellow
"Sunrise on the Hills."

Experiencing the mutations of nature, then, in our own daily history, and vividly so as regards the spiritual half of our being, the names of the divisions of times and seasons become the appropriate metaphors wherein to speak of our varied states of heart and mind. There is no other language for the purpose.

That in nature always most interests us which bears the closest affinity with the feelings we most prize, and those feelings are most prized which yield us our highest satisfaction and solace.

—Leo Hartley Grindon
"Time and Seasons." *Life: Its Nature, Varieties, and Phenomena.*

It is a "law of nature," verifiable by everyday experience, that our already formed convictions, our strong desires, our intent occupation with particular ideas, modify our mental operations to a most marvellous extent, and produce enduring changes in the direction and in the intensity of our intellectual and moral activities.

—Thomas Henry Huxley
"CXXXII". Aphorisms and Reflections.

The general aspect of nature, with its vast power and constant law, has a direct influence to waken reverence and something of awe.

The world of matter affects the imagination: it offers us beauty. How beautiful are the common things about us!

Beauty does not seem requisite to the understanding alone, it is not valuable to man's mere body, certainly it does not seem necessary to the world of matter itself; but it is requisite for the imagination, and this thread of beauty, whose shape and color so witches us, runs through all the cosmic web; it is tied in with the subtle laws of animation, vegetation, motion; it is woven up with attraction, affinity, heat, light, electricity; it is connected into the disposition of the three great parts of the earth, air, water, land, complicated with the subtle chemical character of each; it depends on the structural form of the earth, that on the solar system itself. So when you rejoice in a musical sound, in the sight of flowers, in the bloom on a maiden's cheek, when you look at a charcoal sketch or a bronze statue, when you read a drama of Shakespeare, or listen to an essay of Emerson,—then remember that the relation between matter and mind which made these things possible, depends on the structure of the solar system, and was provided for millions of millions of years before there was a man-child born into the world.

—Theodore Parker
Lessons from the World of Matter and the World of Man.

Finally, brethren, whatsoever things are true, whatsoever things are honest, whatsoever things are just, whatsoever things are pure, whatsoever things are lovely, whatsoever things are of good report; if there be any virtue, and if there be any praise, think on these things.

—Philippians 4:8. *KJV.*

Chapter 4

The Law of Attraction

The Law of Attraction is based on the principle that "like attracts like" in the physical world of nature and in our internal world of mind and consciousness. In the physical world this law manifests in various ways, such as chemical affinity and as Newton's Law of Universal Gravitation.

In our inner world the Law of Attraction maintains that one's thoughts and mental states determine an individual's reality. A person attracts to themselves what they think, whether beneficial or harmful. The law of attraction is revealed through your mind, thoughts, and imagination, and is the tool for creating your reality in the outer world.

The Law of Thought Attraction is one name for the Law, or rather for one manifestation of it. Again I say, your thoughts are real things. They go forth from you in all directions, combining with thoughts of like kind — opposing thoughts of a different character — forming combinations — going where they are attracted — flying away from thought centers opposing them. And your mind attracts the thoughts of others, which have been sent out by them consciously or unconsciously. But it attracts only those thoughts which are in harmony with its own. Like attracts like, and opposites repel opposites, in the world of thought.

—William Walker Atkinson
Thought Vibration: Or, the Law of Attraction
in the Thought World.

I hold it true that thoughts are things;
They're endowed with bodies and breath and wings;
And that we send them forth to fill
The world with good results, or ill.
That which we call our secret thought
Speeds forth to earth's remotest spot,
Leaving its blessings or its woes
Like tracks behind it as it goes.
We build our future, thought by thought,
For good or ill, yet know it not.
Yet, so the universe was wrought.
Thought is another name for fate;
Choose, then, thy destiny and wait.
For love brings love and hate brings hate.

—Henry Van Dyke
"Thoughts Are Things."

This Law of Attraction is neither good nor evil, neither moral nor immoral; it is a neutral law that always flows in conjunction with the desires of the individual; we each choose our own line of growth, and there are as many lines of growth as there are individuals; and although no two of us are exactly alike, yet many of us move along similar lines.

—Charles F. Haanel
Mental Chemistry.

For as he thinketh in his heart, so is he.

—Proverbs 23:7. *KJV.*

What one does and what he thinks, that he becomes.

—Brhadaranyakopanishad
"Union (Yoga)." *The Spirit of the Upanishads;
Or, The Aphorisms of the Wise.*

Every thought tends to become a material thing. Our desires are seed thoughts that have a tendency to sprout and grow and blossom and bear fruit. We are sowing these seeds every day. What shall the harvest be? Each of us today is the result of his past thinking. Later we shall be the result of what we are now thinking. We create our own character, personality and environment by the thought which we originate, or entertain. Thought seeks its own. The law of mental attraction is an exact parallel to the law of atomic affinity. Mental currents are as real as electric, magnetic or heat currents. We attract the currents with which we are in harmony.

—Charles F. Haanel
Mental Chemistry.

Draw nigh to God, and he will draw nigh to you.

—James 4:8. *KJV.*

Grant this we pray Thee, and that all who read,
Or utter noble thoughts, may make them theirs,
And thank God for them, to the betterment
Of their succeeding life.

—Philip James Bailey
"Scene V, A Country Town." *Festus, a Poem.*

The aphorism, "As a man thinketh in his heart so is he," not only embraces the whole of a man's being but is so comprehensive as to reach out to every condition and circumstance of his life. A man is literally what he thinks, his character being the complete sum of all his thoughts.

—James Allen
As A Man Thinketh.

Mind is the Master power that molds and makes,
And Man is Mind, and ever more he takes
The Tool of Thought, and shaping what he wills,
Brings forth a thousand joys, a thousand ills—
He thinks in secret and it comes to pass;
Environment is but his looking-glass.

—James Allen
As A Man Thinketh.

There is in connection with the thought forces what we may term, the drawing power of mind, and the great law operating here is one with that great law of the universe, that like attracts like. We are continually attracting to us from both the seen and the unseen side of life, forces and conditions most akin to those of our own thoughts.

—Ralph Waldo Trine
In Tune with the Infinite.

By the law of attraction our experiences depend upon our mental attitude. Like is attracted to like. Mental attitude is as much the result of character as character is of mental attitude. Each acts and reacts on the other.

—Charles F. Haanel
Mental Chemistry.

A strong purpose holds one down to his task and shuts out a thousand temptations to wander away from his legitimate sphere. A strong purpose does not wait for opportunities; it makes them. It has a magnetic power that draws to itself whatever is kindred, and enlists the support of all the faculties.

—Orison Swett Marden
"The Power of Purpose." *The Consolidated Library, Volume 14.*

Like produces like; a mean, contemptible thought or bearing toward another can never call out love, gratitude, or appreciation. The mind is a magnet and draws from other minds qualities like its own. If we hold others in loving regard, if we are truly interested in their welfare and are really anxious to help them, they quickly respond in like thoughts toward us.

—Orison Swett Marden
"Thought, the Life Builder." *The Consolidated Library, Volume 8.*

Each is building his own world. We both build from within and we attract from without. Thought is the force with which we build, for thoughts are forces. Like builds like and like attracts like.

—Ralph Waldo Trine
In Tune with the Infinite.

Has the naturalist or chemist learned his craft, who has explored the gravity of atoms and the elective affinities, who has not yet discerned the deeper law whereof this is only a partial or approximate statement, namely that like draws to like, and that the goods which belong to you gravitate to you and need not be pursued with pains and cost? Yet is that statement approximate also, and not final. Omnipresence is a higher fact. Not through subtle subterranean channels need friend and fact be drawn to their counterpart, but, rightly considered, these things proceed from the eternal generation of the soul. Cause and effect are two sides of one fact.

—RALPH WALDO EMERSON
"Circles." *Essays, First Series.*

The thought that is most put out brings its corresponding visible element to crystallize about you as surely and literally as the visible bit of copper in solution attracts to it the invisible copper in that solution. A mind always hopeful, confident, courageous, and determined on its set purpose, and keeping itself to that purpose, attracts to itself out of the elements things and powers favorable to that purpose.

—RALPH WALDO TRINE
In Tune with the Infinite.

To accomplish, we must be possessed of earnest desire—must be as confident of ultimate success as we are of the rising of to-morrow's sun—we must have Faith. And we must work out the end with the tools and instruments that will present themselves day by day. We will find that Desire, Confidence,

Faith and Work will not only brush aside the obstacles from our path, but will also begin to assert that wonderful force, as yet so little understood—the Law of Attraction—which will draw to us that which is conducive to our success, be it ideas, people, things, yes, even circumstances.

—WILLIAM WALKER ATKINSON
"The Keynote." *Nuggets of the New Thought.*

Look round our world; behold the chain of love
Combining all below and all above.
See plastic Nature working to this end,
The single atoms each to other tend,
Attract, attracted to, the next in place
Formed and impelled its neighbour to embrace.
See matter next, with various life endued,
Press to one centre still, the general good.

—ALEXANDER POPE
An Essay on Man. Moral Essays and Satires.

Chapter 5

The Law of Inspired Action

The Law of Inspired Action states that real, practical, motivated steps must be taken in order to achieve one's purposes, objectives, and goals. All truly inspirational and instructive literature views worthy objectives and goals as those which are not focused mainly on personal gain and merit, but those which are considered admirable, those in service to others, those for personal fulfilment and growth, those for the development of virtue and character. For purposes, objectives, and goals that are positive, gain and merit may accompany the results, but only consequently, not as the primary motivation.

Inspired actions, or works with a virtuous purpose, can feel effortless, and are satisfying, ego-less, and are in the moment. Advice for inspired actions can come from intuition, the subconscious, or external sources. It has been presumed that The Law of Inspired Action is the key for the manifestation of the Law of Attraction in one's reality. This viewpoint maintains that accomplishing worthwhile goals is a process of co-creation by the individual with the infinite intelligence, or creative force, of the Universe. An individual's actions are essential for this to happen.

To every life there comes a time supreme;
One day, one night, one morning, or one noon,
One freighted hour - one moment opportune,
One rift through which sublime fulfilments gleam;

One time when fate goes tiding with the stream,
One Once in balance 'twixt Too Late, Too Soon,
And ready for the passing instant's boon
That shall in favor tip the wavering beam.

Ah! happy he who, knowing how to wait,
Knows also how to watch and how to stand
On life's broad deck alert, and at the prow,

To seize the happy moment big with fate
From Opportunity's extended hand
When the great clock of Destiny strikes Now!

—Mary Ashley Townsend
"XLVIII." *Distaff and Spindle: Sonnets.*

For as the body without the spirit is dead, so faith without works is dead also.

—James 2:26. *KJV.*

Let us remember how great the ancients were; and especially how the Socratic school holds up to us the source and standard of all life and action, and bids us not indulge in empty speculation, but live and do.

—JOHANN WOLFGANG VON GOETHE
"Literature and Art." *The Maxims and Reflections of Goethe.*

Anything the mind can conceive and believe, it can achieve.

—NAPOLEON HILL
Think and Grow Rich.

Ask, and it shall be given you; seek, and ye shall find; knock, and it shall be opened unto you.

For every one that asketh receiveth; and he that seeketh findeth; and to him that knocketh it shall be opened.

—MATTHEW 7:7-8. *KJV.*

Work thou for pleasure; paint or sing or carve
The thing thou lovest, though the body starve.
Who works for glory misses oft the goal;
Who works for money coins his very soul;
Work for the work's sake, then, and it may be
That these things shall be added unto thee.

—KENYON COX
"Work Thou for Pleasure."

Is there no loving of knowledge, and of art, and of our design, for itself alone? Cannot we please ourselves with performing our work, or gaining truth and power, without being praised for it? I gain my point, I gain all points, if I can reach my companion with any statement which teaches him his own worth. The sum of wisdom is, that the time is never lost that is devoted to work.

—Ralph Waldo Emerson
"Success." *Society and Solitude.*

The promise of delicious youth may fail;
The fair fulfilment of our Summer-time
May wane and wither at its hour of prime;
The gorgeous glow of Hope may swiftly pale;
E'en Love may leave us spite our piteous wail;
The heart, defeated, may desolate climb
To lonely Reason on her height sublime;
But one sure fort no foe can e'er assail.

'Tis thine, O Work, - the joy supreme of thought,
Where feeling, purpose, and long patience meet;
Where in deep silence the ideal wrought
Burgeons from blossoming to fruit complete.
O crowning bliss! O treasure never bought!
All else may perish, thou remainest sweet.

—Mary Clemmer
"The Joy of Work." *Poems of Life and Nature.*

We know that all useful work is the result of sound thought. If we realize that thought itself is the expression of the spirit, we are moved by a sense of duty to give to that spirit the best possible expression of which we are capable, the best chance that it can have, dwelling in imperfect bodies and speaking through imperfect minds such as those we possess.

—Charles F. Haanel
Mental Chemistry.

"Are you in earnest? Seize this very minute:
What you can do, or dream you can, begin it;
Boldness has genius, power, and magic in it.
Only engage and then the mind grows heated;
Begin and then the work will be completed."

— Johann Wolfgang Von Goethe
Faust.

It has been just said, that there is no branch of human work whose constant laws have not close analogy with those which govern every other mode of man's exertion. But, more than this, exactly as we reduce to greater simplicity and surety any one group of these practical laws, we shall find them passing the mere condition of connection or analogy, and becoming the actual expression of some ultimate nerve or fibre of the mighty laws which govern the moral world. However mean or inconsiderable the act, there is something in the well doing of it, which has fellowship with the noblest forms of manly virtue; and the truth, decision, and temperance, which we reverently regard as honorable conditions of the spiritual being, have a representative or derivative influence over the works of the hand, the movements of the frame, and the action of the intellect.

And as thus every action, down even to the drawing of a line or utterance of a syllable, is capable of a peculiar dignity in the manner of it, which we sometimes express by saying it is truly done (as a line or tone is true), so also it is capable of dignity still higher in the motive of it. For there is no action so slight, nor so mean, but it may be done to a great purpose, and ennobled therefore; nor is any purpose so great but that slight actions may help it, and may be so done as to help it much,….

—John Ruskin
"Introductory." *The Seven Lamps of Architecture.*

A servant with this clause
Makes drudgery divine;
Who sweeps a room, as for thy laws,
Makes that and the action fine.

—George Herbert
"Elixir."

Use all your hidden forces. Do not miss
The purpose of this life, and do not wait
For circumstance to mould or change your fate.
In your own self lies Destiny. Let this
Vast truth cast out all fear, all prejudice,
All hesitation. Know that you are great,
Great with divinity. So dominate
Environment, and enter into bliss.

—Ella Wheeler Wilcox
"Attainment." *Poems of Optimism.*

'Work,' it saith to man, 'in every hour, paid or unpaid, see only that thou work, and thou canst not escape the reward: whether thy work be fine or coarse, planting corn, or writing epics, so only it be honest work, done to thine own approbation, it shall earn a reward to the senses as well as to the thought: no matter, how often defeated, you are born to victory. The reward of a thing well done, is to have done it.'

—Ralph Waldo Emerson
"New England Reformers." *Essays, Second Series.*

But he who, with strong body serving mind,
Gives up his mortal powers to worthy work,
Not seeking gain, Arjuna! such an one
Is honourable. Do thine allotted task!
Work is more excellent than idleness;
The body's life proceeds not, lacking work.
There is a task of holiness to do,
Unlike world-binding toil, which bindeth not

The faithful soul; such earthly duty do
Free from desire, and thou shalt well perform
Thy heavenly purpose.

—The Bhagavad-Gita.

'Tis much to know in life our proper task,
Yet more to do, when well we know our work;
Into Life's harvest none are sent to shirk—
Of others' toil the gifts of labor ask;

Only in doing may the arm grow strong,
The mind be strengthened in its own high thought:
And ours—ours only what our hands have wrought,
The sole sure wages that to Toil belong.
Do then thy task, and trust the gods' decree,
That as thy work thy recompense shall be.

—Benjamin Hathaway
"Work." *Art-life And Other Poems.*

Don't do right unwillingly,
And stop to plan and measure;
'Tis working with the heart and soul
That makes our duty pleasure.

—Phoebe Cary
"Now." *The Poetical Works of Alice and Phoebe Cary.*

Did you ever hear of a man who had striven all his life faithfully and singly toward an object and in no measure obtained it? If a man constantly aspires, is he not elevated? Did ever a man try heroism, magnanimity, truth, sincerity, and find that there was no advantage in them, – that it was a vain endeavor?

—Henry David Thoreau
The Writings of Henry David Thoreau.

They err who measure life by years,
With false or thoughtless tongue;
Some hearts grow old before their time;
Others are always young.

'Tis not the number of the lines
On life's fast filling page, -
'Tis not the pulse's added throbs,
Which constitute their age.

Some souls are serfs among the free,
While others nobly thrive;
They stand just where their fathers stood;
Dead, even while they live!

Others, all spirit, heart, and sense;
Theirs the mysterious power
To live in thrills of joy or woe,
A twelvemonth in an hour!

Seize, them the minutes as they pass,
The woof of life is thought!
Warm up the colours; let them glow
With fire and fancy frought.

Live to some purpose; make thy life
A gift of use to thee:
A joy, a good, a golden hope,
A heavenly argosy!

—Bryan Waller Procter
"The Gauge of Life."

For we are not sent into this world to do any thing into which we cannot put our hearts. We have certain work to do for our bread, and that is to be done strenuously; other work to do for our delight, and that is to be done heartily: neither is to be done by halves or shifts, but with a will; and what is not worth this effort is not to be done at all.

—John Ruskin
"The Lamp of Life. XXIV."
The Seven Lamps of Architecture.

Opportunity should never knock at your door to find it bolted. Through the changeful phases of life we are the executors of a will that is greater than our will, and that by this very fact sustains us. Give yourselves, with a good heart, to its service, and let it work through you. Keep your powder dry and your sword burnished!

—Charles Wagner
The Better Way.

A little consideration of what takes place around us every day would show us that a higher law than that of our will regulates events; that our painful labors are unnecessary and fruitless; that only in our easy, simple, spontaneous action are we strong, and by contenting ourselves with obedience we become divine.

—Ralph Waldo Emerson
"Spiritual Laws." *Essays, First Series.*

I think that the majority of those who have met with a greater share of Success by means of the wonderful power of Thought, have met with such Success not by having it fall from the skies, but by following out the ideas, impulses, yes, inspiration, if you will, that have come to them.

The Law will open the door to you, but will not push you in.

And the Law insists upon doing its work in its own good way—not in your way. You may know what you want, but you may not know just the right way to get it, although you think you do.

The Law will give you many a hint, and many a gentle push in the proper direction, but it always leaves you the liberty of choice—the right to refuse. It does not insist upon your love, your Faith; that is, it does not make you love and have Faith, but until you do love and have Faith you are not conscious of the promptings of the Spirit, or, at most, dismiss them as beneath your notice.

—William Walker Atkinson
"How Success Comes." *Nuggets of the New Thought.*

Not enjoyment, and not sorrow,
Is our destined end or way;
But to act, that each to-morrow
Find us farther than to-day.

> —Henry Wadsworth Longfellow
> "A Psalm of Life."

No endeavor is in vain;
Its reward is in the doing,
And the rapture of pursuing
Is the prize the vanquished gain.

> —Henry Wadsworth Longfellow
> "The Wind Over the Chimney."

Not merely to know, but according to thy knowledge, to do, is the destiny of man. "Not for leisurely contemplation of thyself, not to brood over devout sensations, art thou here. Thine action, thine action alone, determines thy worth."

> —Johann Gottlieb Fichte
> *The Destination of Man.*

High hearts are never long without hearing some new call, some distant clarion of God, even in their dreams: and soon they are observed to break up the camp of ease and start on some fresh march of faithful service......

And finally, looking higher still, we find those who never wait till their moral work accumulates, and who reward resolution with no rest; with whom therefore the alternation is instantaneous and constant; who do the good only to see the better and see the better only to achieve it; who are too meek for transport, too faithful for remorse, too earnest for repose; whose worship is action, and whose action ceaseless aspiration.

—JAMES MARTINEAU
Endeavours After the Christian Life.

…. for life affords no higher pleasure than that of surmounting difficulties, passing from one step of success to another, forming new wishes, and seeing them gratified. He that labours in any great or laudable undertaking, has his fatigues first supported by hope, and afterwards rewarded by joy; he is always moving to a certain end, and when he has attained it, an end more distant invites him to a new pursuit.

—SAMUEL JOHNSON
"No. 111." *The Adventurer. (The Works of Samuel Johnson).*

I learned this, at least, by my experiment; that if one advances confidently in the direction of his dreams, and endeavors to live the life which he has imagined, he will meet with a success unexpected in common hours. He will put some things behind, will pass an invisible boundary; new, universal, and more liberal laws will begin to establish themselves around and within him; or the old laws be expanded, and interpreted in his favor in a more liberal sense, and he will live with the license of a higher order of beings. In proportion as he simplifies his life, the laws of the universe will appear less complex, and solitude will not be solitude, nor poverty poverty, nor weakness weakness. If you have built castles in the air, your work need not be lost; that is where they should be. Now put the foundations under them.

—Henry David Thoreau
"Conclusion." *Walden.*

Chapter 6

THE LAW OF PERPETUAL TRANSMUTATION OF ENERGY

The Law of Perpetual Transmutation of Energy is a law of change. Scientific observation and experience show that everything in the universe is constantly moving, evolving, changing, transforming into other states or conditions, whether matter, energy states, thoughts, or ideas. And while the forms of things change continuously, the energy is enduring and indestructible.

This law has many manifestations representing actual change in the energy of the physical world, and changes within the energy of our inner world of emotions, thoughts, feelings, and ideas. Understanding and embracing this mutability is key in aligning with its power and benefit.

Turn, turn, my wheel! All things must change
To something new, to something strange;
Nothing that is can pause or stay;
The moon will wax, the moon will wane,
The mist and cloud will turn to rain,
The rain to mist and cloud again,
To-morrow be to-day.

Turn, turn, my wheel! All life is brief;
What now is bud will soon be leaf,
What now is leaf will soon decay;
The wind blows east, the wind blows west;
The blue eggs in the robin's nest
Will soon have wings and beak and breast,
And flutter and fly away.

—Henry Wadsworth Longfellow
"Keramos." *Keramos and Other Poems.*

All growing ends in fading, all rising ends in falling, all meeting ends in parting —such indeed is the law of this world.

—Yogavasishtha
"The Four-Fold Means." *The Spirit of the Upanishads;*
Or, The Aphorisms of the Wise.

Observe constantly that all things take place by change, and accustom thyself to consider that the nature of the Universe loves nothing so much as to change the things which are to make new things like them. For everything that exists is in a manner the seed of that which will be.

—Marcus Aurelius
The Meditations of Marcus Aurelius.

Nature, thy daughter, ever-changing birth
Of Thee the Great Immutable, to man
Speaks wisdom, is his oracle supreme;
And he who most consults her, is most wise.
Lorenzo, to this heavenly Delphos haste;
And come back all-immortal, all-divine:
Look nature through, 'tis revolution all;
All change; no death. Day follows night; and night
The dying day; stars rise, and set, and rise;
Earth takes th' example. See, the summer gay,
With her green chaplet, and ambrosial flowers,
Droops into pallid autumn: winter grey,
Horrid with frost, and turbulent with storm,
Blows autumn, and his golden fruits, away:
Then melts into the spring: soft spring, with breath
Favonian, from warm chambers of the south,
Recalls the first. All, to re-flourish, fades;
As in a wheel, all sinks, to re-ascend.
Emblems of man, who passes, not expires.

—Edward Young
"Night Sixth." *Night Thoughts, on Life, Death, and Immortality.*

Change is the great lord of the world; time is his agent, which brings all things under his unstaid dominion…

—Owen Felltham
Resolves, Divine, Moral and Political of Owen Felltham.

For as with winter and summer, light and darkness, heat and cold, rain and sunshine, clouds and azure, music and silence, —for even the wind and the waters are still at times, —so with health and sickness, hunger and content, fatigue and vigour; no state or condition is lasting. Down even to the minute and secret phenomena of what the physiologists call ' molecular death,' namely, the continual decay and replacement of the animal tissues, Change is the universal condition of existence. And while so marked a feature of the inanimate world, and of the animal life, infinitely more true of the soul, because of its infinitely higher capabilities and senses. At one moment buoyant with hope, at another depressed by disappointment or misgivings; cheerful to-day, mournful to-morrow; in the course even of a few minutes it will run through a long series of intensest emotions. Change, accordingly, has in all ages been the chosen theme of the moralist and the preacher…..

Well styled by Felltham, "the great lord of the universe," all the best charms of objective nature, and all the noblest attitudes of the intellect and affections owe their being to its magic touch. Incessantly at work, transfiguring, dissolving, and recombining, it makes the physical world one vast kaleidoscope wherein new and unthought-of charms are brought to view with every turn of day and season. Changed, not destroyed, our lament for the beautiful as it glides from out our grasp, is but to lament that brighter things are coming. For there is no truth more sublime than that decay, death, and disappearance are not annihilation, but simply the attendants on change of form.

…the flowers of the summer cease to smile, that the fruits of autumn may step forth. So with the changes of the inner life. For as changes and contrasts are the springs of all our happiness and enjoyment in connection with the external life, as well as productive of the most charming aspects and conditions of nature; so is it from changes in our spiritual states that we acquire true wisdom, and that our affections become invited into their loveliest and most sacred channels. No one, for instance, is capable of truly and heartily sympathizing with the troubles of another, until he has himself been touched by sorrow.

—Leo Hartley Grindon
"Time and Seasons." *Life: Its Nature, Varieties, and Phenomena.*

Nature is a mutable cloud which is always and never the same. She casts the same thought into troops of forms, as a poet makes twenty fables with one moral. Through the bruteness and toughness of matter, a subtle spirit bends all things to its own will.

Nature is an endless combination and repetition of a very few laws. She hums the old well-known air through innumerable variations.

—Ralph Waldo Emerson
"History." *Essays, First Series.*

This let me further add, that Nature knows
No stedfast station, but, or ebbs, or flows:
Ever in motion; she destroys her old,
And casts new figures in another mold.
Ev'n times are in perpetual flux, and run,
Like rivers from their fountain, rolling on,

For time, no more than streams, is at a stay;
The flying hour is ever on her way:
And as the fountain still supplies her store,
The wave behind impels the wave before;
Thus in successive course the minutes run,
And urge their predecessor minutes on,
Till moving, ever new: for former things
Are set aside, like abdicated kings:
And every moment alters what is done,
And innovates some Act, till then unknown.

—Ovid
Metamorphoses, XV.

The handful of soil is a factory thronged with swarms of busy workers; the rusty nail is an aggregation of millions of particles, moving with inconceivable velocity in a dance of infinite complexity yet perfect measure; harmonic with like performances throughout the solar system. If there is good ground for any conclusion, there is such for the belief that the substance of these particles has existed and will exist, that the energy which stirs them has persisted and will persist, without assignable limit, either in the past or the future. Surely, as Heracleitus said of his kitchen with its pots and pans, "Here also are the gods." Little as we have, even yet, learned of the material universe, that little makes for the belief that it is a system of unbroken order and perfect symmetry, of which the form incessantly changes, while the substance and the energy are imperishable.

—Thomas Henry Huxley
"CLXVI". *Aphorisms and Reflections.*

This immutability in the midst of eternal disturbance, this constancy where so many changes are perpetually at work, can only be the result of a wonderful order, of a masterly balance between conflicting influences.

—Georg Hartwig
"Chapter III The Atmospheric Ocean." *The Harmonies of Nature or The Unity of Creation.*

Stars sweep and question not. This is enough
  That life and death and joy and woe abide;
And cause and sequence, and the course of time,
  And Being's ceaseless tide,

Which, ever-changing, runs, linked like a river
  By ripples following ripples, fast or slow—
The same yet not the same—from far-off fountain
  To where its waters flow

Into the seas. These, steaming to the Sun,
  Give the lost wavelets back in cloudy fleece
To trickle down the hills, and glide again;
  Having no pause or peace.

This is enough to know, the phantasms are;
  The Heavens, Earths, Worlds, and changes changing them
A mighty whirling wheel of strife and stress
  Which none can stay or stem.

—Edwin Arnold
The Light of Asia: Or, The Great Renunciation.

In Change, therefore, there is nothing terrible, nothing supernatural: on the contrary, it lies in the very essence of our lot and life in this world. Today is not yesterday: we ourselves change; how can our Works and Thoughts, if they are always to be the fittest, continue always the same? Change, indeed, is painful; yet ever needful; and if Memory have its force and worth, so also has Hope.

—Thomas Carlyle
"Characteristics."

We are as clouds that veil the midnight moon;
How restlessly they speed, and gleam, and quiver,
Streaking the darkness radiantly!— yet soon
Night closes round, and they are lost for ever:
Or like forgotten lyres, whose dissonant strings
Give various response to each varying blast,
To whose frail frame no second motion brings
One mood or modulation like the last.
We rest.— A dream has power to poison sleep;
We rise.— One wandering thought pollutes the day;
We feel, conceive or reason, laugh or weep;
Embrace fond woe, or cast our cares away:
It is the same!— For, be it joy or sorrow,
The path of its departure still is free:
Man's yesterday may ne'er be like his morrow;
Nought may endure but Mutability.

—Percy Bysshe Shelley
"Mutability."

Some things are hurrying into existence, and others are hurrying out of it; and of that which is coming into existence part is already extinguished. Motions and changes are continually renewing the world, just as the uninterrupted course of time is always renewing the infinite duration of ages.

Nature which governs the whole will soon change all things thou seest, and out of their substance will make other things, and again other things from the substance of them, in order that the world may be ever new.

—Marcus Aurelius
The Meditations of Marcus Aurelius.

In nature every moment is new; the past is always swallowed and forgotten; the coming only is sacred. Nothing is secure but life, transition, the energizing spirit.

—Ralph Waldo Emerson
"Circles." *Essays, First Series.*

In the degree that we employ ourselves we acquire Power. As nature, ever shifting and transforming, is most beautiful and delicious when it is not strictly either spring, or summer, or autumn; morning, noon, or night; so all the potency we ever possess is referable to our moments of action, or when we are experiencing or effecting Changes; the period of transition is that in which Power is developed; to acquire and to wield it we must be for ever seeking to quit the state we are in, and rise into a higher one. Power, accordingly, which is only Life under another name, is resolvable, essentially, into progression. It never consists in the having been, but always in the becoming.

—Leo Hartley Grindon
"Chapter XVIII. Life Realized by Activity. — Action the Law of Happiness." *Life: Its Nature, Varieties, and Phenomena.*

Whoever observes the world, and the order of it, will find all the motions in it to be only vicissitudes of falling and rising; nothing extinguished, and even those things which seem to us to perish are in truth but changed. The seasons go and return, day and night follow in their courses, the heavens roll, and Nature goes on with her work: all things succeed in their turns, storms and calms; the law of Nature will have it so, which we must follow and obey, accounting all things that are done to be well done…

— Lucius Annaeus Seneca
"Of a Happy Life."

Moved by invisible power, the clouds upsoar
Like metals hued gold, bronze, white, silver-gray,
And lift a vast aerial array
Of moisture, fire, and wind the hot hills o'er:

The forests stir to primal depths once more,
And vivid lightnings flash about the day
Like knives by Indian jugglers thrown at play,
While near and nearer threatening thunders roar.

Now, motion, tumult, and a flooding rain,
That blots the world out for a noisy while,
Then, sudden sunshine and the storm has ceased;

But with the heights the luminous mists remain,
And 'neath their haze the mountains stand and smile,
All veiled like beauties of the haremed East.

—MARY ASHLEY TOWNSEND
"XV." *Distaff and Spindle: Sonnets.*

Often think of the rapidity with which things pass by and disappear, both the things which are and the things which are produced. For substance is like a river in a continual flow, and the activities of things are in constant change, and the causes work in infinite varieties; and there is hardly anything which stands still. And consider this which is near to thee, this boundless abyss of the past and of the future in which all things disappear.

—MARCUS AURELIUS
The Meditations of Marcus Aurelius.

As Providence has made the human soul an active being, always impatient for novelty, and struggling for something yet unenjoyed with unwearied progression, the world seems to have been eminently adapted to this disposition of the mind; it is formed to raise expectations by constant vicissitudes, and to obviate satiety by perpetual change.

Wherever we turn our eyes, we find something to revive our curiosity, and engage our attention. In the dusk of the morning we watch the rising of the sun, and see the day diversify the clouds, and open new prospects in its gradual advance. After a few hours, we see the shades lengthen, and the light decline, till the sky is resigned to a multitude of shining orbs different from each other in magnitude and splendour. The earth varies its appearance as we move upon it; the woods offer their shades, and the fields their harvests; the hill flatters with an extensive view, and the valley invites with shelter, fragrance, and flowers.

—Samuel Johnson
"No. 80." *The Rambler. Vol. 1.*
(The Works of Samuel Johnson).

When, in rosy chariot drawn,
Phœbus 'gins to light the dawn,
By his flaming beams assailed,
Every glimmering star is paled.
When the grove, by Zephyrs fed,
With rose-blossom blushes red;—
Doth rude Auster breathe thereon,
Bare it stands, its glory gone.
Smooth and tranquil lies the deep

While the winds are hushed in sleep.
Soon, when angry tempests lash,
Wild and high the billows dash.
Thus if Nature's changing face
Holds not still a moment's space,
Fleeting deem man's fortunes; deem
Bliss as transient as a dream.
One law only standeth fast:
Things created may not last.

—Boethius
"Song III, Book II." *The Consolation of Philosophy of Boethius.*

And the more we learn of the nature of things, the more evident is it that what we call rest is only unperceived activity; that seeming peace is silent but strenuous battle. In every part, at every moment, the state of the cosmos is the expression of a transitory adjustment of contending forces; a scene of strife, in which all the combatants fall in turn. What is true of each part is true of the whole. Natural knowledge tends more and more to the conclusion that "all the choir of heaven and furniture of the earth" are the transitory forms of parcels of cosmic substance wending along the road of evolution, from nebulous potentiality, through endless growths of sun and planet and satellite; through all varieties of matter; through infinite diversities of life and thought; possibly, through modes of being of which we neither have a conception, nor are competent to form any, back to the indefinable latency from which they arose. Thus the most obvious attribute of the cosmos is its impermanence. It assumes the aspect not so much of a permanent entity as of a changeful process, in which naught endures save the flow of energy and the rational order which pervades it.

—Thomas Henry Huxley
"CCXL." *Aphorisms and Reflections.*

By ceaseless action, all that is subsists.
Constant rotation of the unwearied wheel
That Nature rides upon, maintains her health,
Her beauty, her fertility. She dreads
An instant's pause, and lives but while she moves.
Its own revolvency upholds the world.
Winds from all quarters agitate the air,
And fit the limpid element for use,
Else noxious: oceans, rivers, lakes, and streams
All feel the freshening impulse, and are cleansed
By restless undulation: even the oak
Thrives by the rude concussion of the storm:
He seems indeed indignant, and to feel
The impression of the blast with proud disdain,
Frowning as if in his unconscious arm
He held the thunder. But the monarch owes
His firm stability to what he scorns,
More fixed below, the more disturbed above.
The law, by which all creatures else are bound,
Binds man the lord of all. Himself derives
No mean advantage from a kindred cause,
From strenuous toil his hours of sweetest ease.

—William Cowper
"The Task." *The Task and Other Poems.*

In incessant vibration the universal work is performed. Matter is being constantly played upon by energy and countless forms and numberless varieties result, and yet even the forms and varieties are not permanent. They begin to change the moment they are created, and from them are born innumerable forms, which in turn change, and give rise to newer forms, and so on and on, in infinite succession. Nothing is permanent in the world of forms, and yet the great Reality is unchangeable. Forms are but appearances—they come, they go, but the Reality is eternal and unchangeable.

—Yogi Ramacharaka
*Hatha Yoga or the Yogi Philosophy
of Physical Well-being.*

*Into the sunshine,
Full of the light,
Leaping and flashing
From morn till night!*

*Into the moonlight,
Whiter than snow,
Waving so flower-like
When the winds blow!*

*Into the starlight,
Rushing in spray,
Happy at midnight,
Happy by day!*

Ever in motion,
Blithesome and cheery.
Still climbing heavenward,
Never aweary; —

Glad of all weathers,
Still seeming best,
Upward or downward,
Motion thy rest; —

Full of a nature
Nothing can tame,
Changed every moment,
Ever the same; —

Ceaseless aspiring,
Ceaseless content,
Darkness or sunshine
Thy element; —

Glorious fountain!
Let my heart be
Fresh, changeful, constant,
Upward, like thee!

—JAMES RUSSELL LOWELL
"The Fountain." *Poems of James Russell Lowell.*

Nature! We are surrounded by her and locked in her clasp: powerless to leave her, and powerless to come closer to her. Unasked and unwarned she takes us up into the whirl of her dance, and hurries on with us till we are weary and fall from her arms.

She creates new forms without end: what exists now, never was before; what was, comes not again; all is new and yet always the old.

There is constant life in her, motion and development; and yet she remains where she was. She is eternally changing, nor for a moment does she stand still. Of rest she knows nothing, and to all stagnation she has affixed her curse. She is steadfast; her step is measured, her exceptions rare, her laws immutable.

—Johann Wolfgang Von Goethe
"Nature: Aphorisms." *The Maxims and Reflections of Goethe.*

The day wore on, and all these bright colours subsided, and assumed a quieter tint, like young hopes softened down by time, or youthful features by degrees resolving into the calm and serenity of age. But they were scarcely less beautiful in their slow decline, than they had been in their prime; for nature gives to every time and season some beauties of its own; and from morning to night, as from the cradle to the grave, is but a succession of changes so gentle and easy, that we can scarcely mark their progress.

—Charles Dickens
The Life and Adventures of Nicholas Nickleby.

Chapter 7

The Law of Cause and Effect

The Law of Cause and Effect states that any action in the universe creates a subsequent reaction, that every effect has a cause. In the larger nature of things there is a collective aspect present in this law; a "cause" can have multiple interdependent elements or components. In the planting of a seed and growth of the plant, many prior actions caused the creation and planting of the seed, and the "effect," or actual growth of the plant, is the result of many interdependent scientific causes (genetics, moisture, sunlight, and so on).

This principle in the Bible is stated as "sowing and reaping", and in Buddhism as "Dependent Origination." This law has parallels in our human condition. It maintains that everything results from dependence upon many other things. The physical world can affect and influence our inner mental world, and our inner mental world of emotions, feelings, and thoughts can influence how we see and engage with our outer physical world.

Every Cause has its Effect; every Effect has its Cause; everything happens according to Law; Chance is but a name for Law not recognized; there are many planes of causation, but nothing escapes the Law.

—"The Seven Hermetic Principles."
The Kybalion.

Then from whate'er we can to sense produce
Common and plain, or wondrous and abstruse,
From Nature's constant or eccentric laws,
The thoughtful soul this general influence draws,
That an effect must pre-suppose a cause;
And while she does her upward flight sustain,
Touching each link of the continued chain,
At length she is obliged and forced to see
A first, a source, a life, a Deity;
What has for ever been, and must for ever be.

—Matthew Prior
"Knowledge. Book 1." *Solomon on the Vanity of the World. A Poem. In Three Books.*

……and cause and effect is as absolute and undeviating in the hidden realm of thought as in the world of visible and material things.

—James Allen
As a Man Thinketh.

…. for whatsoever a man soweth, that shall he also reap.

—Galatians 6:7. *KJV.*

Oh! what a tangled web we weave
When first we practise to deceive!

—Sir Walter Scott
"Canto VI. Stanza 17." *Marmion.*

This being, that becomes.
From the arising of this, that arises.
This not being, that does not become.
From the ceasing of this, that ceases.

—"Majjhima-Nikaya ii.32"
The Middle-length Discourses of the Buddha.

Whatsoever doth happen in the world, is, in the course of nature, as usual and ordinary as a rose in the spring, and fruit in summer. Of the same nature is sickness and death; slander, and lying in wait, and whatsoever else ordinarily doth unto fools use to be occasion either of joy or sorrow. That, whatsoever it is, that comes after, doth always very naturally, and as it were familiarly, follow upon that which was before. For thou must consider the things of the world, not as a loose independent number, consisting merely of necessary events; but as a discreet connection of things orderly and harmoniously disposed. There is then to be seen in the things of the world, not a bare succession, but an admirable correspondence and affinity.

—Marcus Aurelius
The Meditations of Marcus Aurelius.

In the series of things, those which follow are always aptly fitted to those which have gone before: for this series is not like a mere enumeration of disjointed things, which has only a necessary sequence, but it is a rational connection: and as all existing things are arranged together harmoniously, so the things which come into existence exhibit no mere succession, but a certain wonderful relationship.

—Marcus Aurelius
The Meditations of Marcus Aurelius.

Every act rewards itself, or, in other words integrates itself, in a twofold manner; first in the thing, or in real nature; and secondly in the circumstance, or in apparent nature. Men call the circumstance the retribution. The causal retribution is in the thing and is seen by the soul. The retribution in the circumstance is seen by the understanding; it is inseparable from the thing, but is often spread over a long time and so does not become distinct until after many years. The specific stripes may follow late after the offence, but they follow because they accompany it. Crime and punishment grow out of one stem. Punishment is a fruit that unsuspected ripens within the flower of the pleasure which concealed it. Cause and effect, means and ends, seed and fruit, cannot be severed; for the effect already blooms in the cause, the end preexists in the means, the fruit in the seed.

—Ralph Waldo Emerson
"Compensation." *Essays, First Series.*

Then one of the judges of the city stood forth and said, Speak to us of Crime and Punishment.
And he answered, saying:
It is when your spirit goes wandering upon the wind,
That you, alone and unguarded, commit a wrong unto others and therefore unto yourself.
And for that wrong committed must you knock and wait a while unheeded at the gate of the blessed.
Like the ocean is your god-self;
It remains for ever undefiled.
And like the ether it lifts but the winged.
Even like the sun is your god-self;
It knows not the ways of the mole nor seeks it the holes of the serpent. But your god-self dwells not alone in your being. Much in you is still man, and much in you is not yet man,

But a shapeless pigmy that walks asleep in the mist searching for its own awakening.
And of the man in you would I now speak.
For it is he and not your god-self nor the pigmy in the mist, that knows crime and the punishment of crime.

—Kahlil Gibran
The Prophet.

The study of cause and effect, while it lessens the painfulness of life, adds to life's picturesqueness. The man to whom evolution is but a name looks at the sea as a grandiose, monotonous spectacle, which he can witness in August for three shillings third-class return. The man who is imbued with the idea of development, of continuous cause and effect, perceives in the sea an element which in the day-before-yesterday of geology was vapour, which yesterday was boiling, and which to-morrow will inevitably be ice. He perceives that a liquid is merely something on its way to be solid, and he is penetrated by a sense of the tremendous, changeful picturesqueness of life. Nothing will afford a more durable satisfaction than the constantly cultivated appreciation of this. It is the end of all science.

—Arnold Bennett
How to Live on Twenty-four Hours a Day.

The whole of human life is cause and effect; there is no such thing in it as chance, nor is there even in all the wide universe. Are we not satisfied with whatever comes into our lives? The thing to do, then, is not to spend time in railing against the imaginary something we create and call fate, but to look to the within, and change the causes at work there, in order that things of a different nature may come, for there will come exactly what we cause to come. This is true not only of the physical body, but of all phases and conditions of life.

—Ralph Waldo Trine
In Tune with the Infinite.

With the means all right, the end must come. We forget that it is the cause that produces the effect; the effect cannot come by itself; and unless the causes are exact, proper, and powerful, the effect will not be produced. Once the ideal is chosen and the means determined, we may almost let go the ideal, because we are sure it will be there, when the means are perfected. When the cause is there, there is no more difficulty about the effect, the effect is bound to come. If we take care of the cause, the effect will take care of itself. The realization of the ideal is the effect. The means are the cause: attention to the means, therefore, is the great secret of life.

—Swami Vivekananda
"Volume 2." *The Complete Works of Swami Vivekananda.*

She made answer: 'I will accede to thy request;' and forthwith she thus began: 'If chance be defined as a result produced by random movement without any link of causal connection, I roundly affirm that there is no such thing as chance at all, and consider the word to be altogether without meaning, except as a symbol of the thing designated. What place can be left for random action, when God constraineth all things to order? For "ex nihilo nihil" is sound doctrine which none of the ancients gainsaid, although they used it of material substance, not of the efficient principle; this they laid down as a kind of basis for all their reasonings concerning nature. Now, if a thing arise without causes, it will appear to have arisen from nothing. But if this cannot be, neither is it possible for there to be chance in accordance with the definition just given.'

We may, then, define chance as being an unexpected result flowing from a concurrence of causes where the several factors had some definite end. But the meeting and concurrence of these causes arises from that inevitable chain of order which, flowing from the fountain-head of Providence, disposes all things in their due time and place.'

—BOETHIUS
"1, Book V." *The Consolation of Philosophy of Boethius*

So use all that is called Fortune. Most men gamble with her, and gain all, and lose all, as her wheel rolls. But do thou leave as unlawful these winnings, and deal with Cause and Effect, the chancellors of God. In the Will work and acquire, and thou hast chained the wheel of Chance, and shalt sit hereafter out of fear from her rotations.

—RALPH WALDO EMERSON
"Self-Reliance." *Essays, First Series.*

There is a process of seed-sowing in the mind and life a spiritual sowing which leads to a harvest according to the kind of seed sown. Thoughts, words, and acts are seeds sown, and, by the inviolable law of things, they produce after their kind. He who would be blest, let him scatter blessings. He who would be happy, let him consider the happiness of others. So in life, we get by giving; we grow rich by scattering.

—James Allen
Above Life's Turmoil.

You reap what you sow - not something else, but that. An act of love makes the soul more loving. A deed of humbleness deepens humbleness. The thing reaped is the very thing sown, multiplied a hundred-fold. You have sown a seed of life; you reap life everlasting.

—Frederick William Robertson
"First Series. Sermon 14."
Sermons Preached at Brighton.

That which ye sow ye reap. See yonder fields
The sesamum was sesamum, the corn
Was corn. The Silence and the Darkness knew!
So is a man's fate born.

He cometh, reaper of the things he sowed,
Sesamum, corn, so much cast in past birth;
And so much weed and poison-stuff, which mar
Him and the aching earth.

If he shall labour rightly, rooting these,
And planting wholesome seedlings where they grew,
Fruitful and fair and clean the ground shall be,
And rich the harvest due.

—Edwin Arnold
The Light of Asia: Or, The Great Renunciation.

Since everything then is cause and effect, dependent and supporting, mediate and immediate, and all is held together by a natural though imperceptible chain, which binds together things most distant and most different, I hold it equally impossible to know the parts without knowing the whole, and to know the whole without knowing the parts in detail.

—Blaise Pascal
Pensées (Thoughts).

There is not in the scale of nature a more inseparable connection of cause and effect, than in the case of happiness and virtue; nor anything that more naturally produces the one, or more necessarily presupposes the other.

All the actions of our lives ought to be governed with respect to good and evil: and it is only reason that distinguishes; by which reason we are in such manner influenced, as if a ray of the Divinity were dipt in a mortal body, and that is the perfection of mankind.

—Lucius Annaeus Seneca
"Of a Happy Life."

It is notorious that, to the unthinking mass of mankind, nine-tenths of the facts of life do not suggest the relation of cause and effect; and they practically deny the existence of any such relation by attributing them to chance. Few gamblers but would stare if they were told that the falling of a die on a particular face is as much the effect of a definite cause as the fact of its falling; it is a proverb that "the wind bloweth where it listeth"; and even thoughtful men usually receive with surprise the suggestion, that the form of the crest of every wave that breaks, wind-driven, on the seashore, and the direction of every particle of foam that flies before the gale, are the exact effects of definite causes; and, as such, must be capable of being determined, deductively, from the laws of motion and the properties of air and water. So again, there are large numbers of highly intelligent persons who rather pride themselves on their fixed belief that our volitions have no cause; or that the will causes itself, which is either the same thing, or a contradiction in terms.

—Thomas Henry Huxley
"CLVI". *Aphorisms and Reflections.*

If man was to judge of causes by their effects, there would be no small causes in the universe. In a Nature where every thing is connected, where every thing acts and re-acts, moves and changes, composes and decomposes, forms and destroys, there is not an atom which does not play an important part—that does not occupy a necessary station; there is not an imperceptible particle, however minute, which, placed in convenient circumstances, does not operate the most prodigious effects.

They are, however, these motives, weak as they may appear to be, these springs, so pitiful in his eyes, which according to her necessary laws, suffice in the hands of Nature to move the universe.

Thus, imperceptible causes, concealed in the bosom of Nature, until the moment their action is displayed, frequently decide the fate of man.

—Baron d'Holbach (Paul-Henri Thiry)
"Chapter XII." *The System of Nature, Or, Laws of the Moral and Physical World.*

To the seeing mind nature presents a series, an infinite series, of logical sequences; cause and effect are inseparably joined, and things could in no wise be other than what they are.

Science has banished the arbitrary, the miraculous, the exceptional, from nature, and instead of these things has revealed order, system, and the irrefragable logic of cause and effect. Instead of good and bad spirits contending with one another, it reveals an inevitable beneficence and a steady upward progress. It shows that the universe is made of one stuff, and that no atom can go amiss or lose its way.

The benevolence of Providence is seen in this general, inevitable course of nature. Right actions meet with their reward; health and wholeness are possible; deal fairly and squarely with Nature, and you always get the worth of your money. We know the conditions of disease; we know the conditions of health. The ways of the Eternal are appointed, and we may find them out.

Truly to obey the will of God is our salvation, but we must look for this will, not in some book or creed, but in the order of the universe, in the sequence of cause and effect.

—John Burroughs
"All's Right With The World." *Leaf and Tendril.*

Chapter 8

The Law of Compensation

The Law of Compensation is based on the observation that there is an equity, a balance, a dualistic aspect in life, that as you "give, and it shall be given unto you." Additionally, this concept of reciprocity in the world is interrelated with the Law of Cause and Effect, the Law of Correspondence, and the Law of Polarity. The reciprocal nature of this law has similarities to some aspects of the theory of karma in Hinduism and Buddhism.

This principle of equilibrium or equipoise is present in the natural world and in the human condition. This spiritual principle affirms that the virtues that we practice towards others, such as generosity, sympathy, love, gratitude, patience, tolerance, and kindness, will be returned to us in time, in one way or another, as the natural order of things.

Thus is the universe alive. All things are moral. That soul, which within us is a sentiment, outside of us is a law. We feel its inspiration; out there in history we can see its fatal strength. "It is in the world, and the world was made by it." Justice is not postponed. A perfect equity adjusts its balance in all parts of life. —the dice of God are always loaded. The world looks like a multiplication table, or a mathematical equation, which, turn it how you will, balances itself. Take what figure you will, its exact value, nor more nor less, still returns to you. Every secret is told, every crime is punished, every virtue rewarded, every wrong redressed, in silence and certainty. What we call retribution is the universal necessity by which the whole appears wherever a part appears.

—Ralph Waldo Emerson
"Compensation." *Essays, First Series.*

This does not mean that duty always is easy; it does not deny the self-sacrifice which right living involves. Everything worth while in the intellectual or moral life must be bought and paid for by giving up irreconcilable habits and indulgences.

—Harry Emerson Fosdick
Twelve Tests of Character.

The sweetest lives are those to duty wed,
Whose deeds, both great and small,
Are close knit strands of an unbroken thread,
Whose love ennobles all.
The world may sound no trumpet, ring no bells;
The book of life, the slurring record tells.
Thy love shall chant its own beatitudes,
After its own life-working. A child's kiss
Set on thy singing lips shall make thee glad;
A poor man served by thee shall make thee rich;

A sick man helped by thee shall make thee strong;
Thou shalt be served thyself by every sense
Of service thou renderest.

—Elizabeth Barrett Browning
"Reward of Service."

Good and ill are universally intermingled and confounded; happiness and misery, wisdom and folly, virtue and vice. Nothing is pure and entirely of a piece. All advantages are attended with disadvantages. An universal compensation prevails in all conditions of being and existence.

—David Hume
Essays Moral, Political, and Literary.

All conditions and experiences that come to us do so for our benefit. Difficulties and obstacles will continue to come until we absorb their wisdom and gather from them the essentials of further growth. That we reap what we sow, is mathematically exact. We gain permanent strength exactly to the extent of the effort required to overcome our difficulties.

—Charles F. Haanel
Mental Chemistry.

Consider, whatever be thy fate, that it might and ought to have been worse,
And that it lieth in thy hand to gather even blessing from afflictions:

Bethink thee, wherefore were they sent? and hath not use blunted their keenness?
Need hope, and patience, and courage, be strangers to the meanest hovel?
Thou art in an evil case, it were cruel to deny to thee compassion, But there is not unmitigated ill in the sharpest of this world's sorrows:
I touch not the sore of thy guilt; but of human griefs I counsel thee,
Cast off the weakness of regret, and gird thee to redeem thy loss:
Thou hast gained, in the furnace of affliction, self-knowledge, patience, and humility,
And these be as precious ore, that waiteth the skill of the coiner:
Despise not the blessings of adversity, nor the gain thou hast earned so hardly,
And now thou hast drained the bitter, take heed that thou lose not the sweet.

—Martin Farquhar Tupper
"Of Compensation." *Proverbial Philosophy: A Book of Thoughts and Arguments.*

What is it we look for in the landscape, in sunsets and sunrises, in the sea and the firmament? what but a compensation for the cramp and pettiness of human performances? We bask in the day, and the mind finds somewhat as great as itself. In Nature, all is large, massive repose.

—Ralph Waldo Emerson
"Success." *Society and Solitude.*

If only in thine heart there be
Some depth of earnest gratitude
For life's great bounties unto thee,
Though pain will come and fears intrude,
Thou canst not wholly miss the crown
Of those by heaven accounted blessed:
Patience will bring a healing down,
And peace will give the spirit rest.

—Leslie Pinckney Hill
"Compensation." *The Wings of Oppression.*

Then he who looks at all at the working of the grand principle of compensation which holds all nature in equipoise, cannot long remain a stranger to the meaning of the beautiful parable of the prodigal son, and the joy over finding the one lost piece of silver. It is no arbitrary kindness, no generosity of the ruling powers, which causes that there be more joy in heaven over the one that returns, than over ninety and nine that never strayed. It is the inevitable working of a spiritual law that he who has been groping in darkness must feel the light most keenly, best know how to prize it—he who has long been exiled from the truth seize it with the most earnest grasp, live in it with the deepest joy.

—Margaret Fuller
"Late Aspirations." *Life Without and Life Within, Or, Reviews, Narratives, Essays, and Poems.*

Give, and it shall be given unto you; good measure, pressed down, and shaken together, and running over, shall men give into your bosom. For with the same measure that ye mete withal it shall be measured to you again.

—L<small>UKE</small> 6:38. *KJV.*

Draw nigh to God, and he will draw nigh to you.

—J<small>AMES</small> 4:8. *KJV.*

Give thy heart's best treasures—
From fair Nature learn;
Give thy love—and ask not,
Wait not a return!
And the more thou spendest
From thy little store,
With a double bounty,
God will give thee more.

—A<small>DELAIDE</small> A<small>NNE</small> P<small>ROCTER</small>
"Give." *Legends and Lyrics: A Book of Verses.*

A forest dark, bewildering,
This life we wander through;
Praise God for those who work and sing,
For both we have to do—
Our greater mission not to win
The thing we most desire,
But more to keep, through care and sin,
Our hearts with love afire.

For there are others on the road,
The dark and misty trail,
And we who bear the lighter load
Must help the ones who fail;
And, helping on the weary soul
Who stumbles by alone,
Thus we, in striving for his goal,
Shall come upon our own.

—Douglas Malloch
"Sympathy." *In Forest Land.*

The tone in which we speak to the world, the world speaks to us. Give your best and you will get the best in return. Give in heaping measure and in heaping measure it shall be returned. We all get our due sooner or later, in one form or another. "Be not weary in well doing;" the reward will surely come, if not in worldly goods, then in inward satisfaction, grace of spirit, peace of mind.

—John Burroughs
"An Outlook Upon Life." *Leaf and Tendril.*

Therefore all things whatsoever ye would that men should do to you, do ye even so to them: for this is the law and the prophets.

—Matthew 7:12. *KJV.*

When one cultivates to the utmost the principles of his nature, and exercises them on the principle of reciprocity, he is not far from the path. What you do not like when done to yourself, do not do to others.

—The Doctrine of the Mean.
(Confucianism).

However meagre be my worldly wealth,
Let me give something that shall aid my kind—
A word of courage, or a thought of health,
Dropped as I pass for troubled hearts to find.
Let me to-night look back across the span
'Twixt dawn and dark, and to my conscience say—
Because of some good act to beast or man—
"The world is better that I lived to-day."

—Ella Wheeler Wilcox
"Morning Prayer." Poems of Power.

My cot was down by a cypress grove,
And I sat by my window the whole night long,
And heard well up from the deep dark wood
A mocking-bird's passionate song.

And I thought of myself so sad and lone,
And my life's cold winter that knew no spring;
Of my mind so weary and sick and wild,
Of my heart too sad to sing.

But e'en as I listened the mock-bird's song,
A thought stole into my saddened heart,

*And I said, "I can cheer some other soul
By a carol's simple art."*

*For oft from the darkness of hearts and lives
Come songs that brim with joy and light,
As out of the gloom of the cypress grove
The mocking-bird sings at night.*

*So I sang a lay for a brother's ear
In a strain to soothe his bleeding heart
And he smiled at the sound of my voice and lyre,
Though mine was a feeble art.*

*But at his smile I smiled in turn,
And into my soul there came a ray:
In trying to soothe another's woes
Mine own had passed away.*

—Paul Laurence Dunbar
"The Lesson." Lyrics of Lowly Life.

Let us not, then, be afraid to give. The more we give, the fuller shall be our life. Let us not be deluded by the world of separateness, where everything grows less as we give it. If I had gold, my store would lessen with every coin that I gave away, but that is not so with the things of the spirit. The more we give, the more we have; each act of giving makes us a larger reservoir.

—Annie Besant
The Meaning and Method of the Spiritual Life.

The law, by which all creatures else are bound,
Binds man the lord of all. Himself derives
No mean advantage from a kindred cause,
From strenuous toil his hours of sweetest ease.

—WILLIAM COWPER
"The Task." *The Task and Other Poems.*

This is its work upon the things ye see,
The unseen things are more; men's hearts and minds,
The thoughts of peoples and their ways and wills,
Those, too, the great Law binds.
Unseen it helpeth ye with faithful hands,
Unheard it speaketh stronger than the storm.
Pity and Love are man's because long stress
Moulded blind mass to form.

It will not be contemned of any one;
Who thwarts it loses, and who serves it gains;
The hidden good it pays with peace and bliss,
The hidden ill with pains.

It seeth everywhere and marketh all
Do right—it recompenseth! do one wrong—
The equal retribution must be made,
Though DHARMA tarry long.

—EDWIN ARNOLD
The Light of Asia: Or, The Great Renunciation.

Yet how do you know what you may lose by neglecting this duty, which you think so trifling, or the blessing which its faithful performance may bring? Be sure that if you do your very best in that which is laid upon you daily, you will not be left without sufficient help when some weightier occasion arises.

—Pere Jean Nicolas Grou
The Hidden Life of the Soul.

The daily round of duty is full of probation and of discipline; it trains the will, heart, and conscience. To be holy we need not to be prophets or apostles. The commonest life may be full of perfection. The duties of home are a discipline for the ministries of heaven.

—Henry Edward Manning
Sermons, Volume the Fourth.

Therefore, thy task prescribed
With spirit unattached gladly perform,
Since in performance of plain duty man
Mounts to his highest bliss.

—The Bhagavad-Gita.

The wings of Time are black and white,
Pied with morning and with night.
Mountain tall and ocean deep
Trembling balance duly keep.
In changing moon, in tidal wave,
Glows the feud of Want and Have.

Gauge of more and less through space
Electric star and pencil plays.
The lonely Earth amid the balls
That hurry through the eternal halls,
A makeweight flying to the void,
Supplemental asteroid,
Or compensatory spark,
Shoots across the neutral Dark.

Man's the elm, and Wealth the vine,
Stanch and strong the tendrils twine;
Through the frail ringlets thee deceive,
None from its stock that vine can reave.
Fear not, then, thou child infirm,
There's no god dare wrong a worm.
Laurel crowns cleave to deserts,
And power to him who power exerts;
Hast not thy share? On winged feet,
Lo! it rushes thee to meet;
And all that Nature made thy own,
Floating in air or pent in stone,
Will rive the hills and swim the sea,
And, like thy shadow, follow thee.

—Ralph Waldo Emerson
"Compensation." *Essays, First Series.*

.... that answer all must give
For all things done amiss or wrongfully,
Alone, each for himself, reckoning with that
The fixed arithmic of the universe,
Which meteth good for good and ill for ill,

Measure for measure, unto deeds, words, thoughts;
Watchful, aware, implacable, unmoved;
Making all futures fruits of all the pasts.

—Edwin Arnold
The Light of Asia: Or, The Great Renunciation.

A flower more sacred than far-seen success
Perfumes my solitary path; I find
Sweet compensation in my humbleness,
And reap the harvest of a tranquil mind.

—John Townsend Trowbridge
"Twoscore and Ten." *A Home Idyl: And Other Poems.*

Equal is the government of heaven in allotting pleasures among men,
And just the everlasting law, that hath wedded happiness to virtue:

Just, and strong, and opportune is the moral rule of God;
Ripe in its times, firm in its judgments, equal in the measure of its gifts:
Yet men, scanning the surface, count the wicked happy,
Nor heed the compensating peace, which gladdeneth the good in his afflictions.

Pain addeth zest unto pleasure, and teacheth the luxury of health;
There is a joy in sorrow, which none but a mourner can know:
Madness hath imaginary bliss, and most men have no more;

Age hath its quiet calm, and youth enjoyeth not for haste:
Daily, in the midst of its beatitude, the righteous soul is vexed;
And even the misery of guilt doth attain to the bliss of pardon.

But, as the water from a fountain riseth and sinketh to its level,
Ceaselessly toileth justice to equalize the lots of men:
For, habit and hope and ignorance, and the being but one of a multitude,
And strength of reason in the sage, and dulness of feeling in the fool,
And the light elasticity of courage, and the calm resignation of meekness,
And the stout endurance of decision, and the weak carelessness of apathy,
And helps invisible but real, and ministerings not unfelt,
Angelic aid with worldly discomfiture, bodily loss with the soul's gain,
Secret griefs, and silent joys, thorns in the flesh, and cordials for the spirit,
(—Short of the insuperable barrier dividing innocence from guilt,—)
Go far to level all things, by the gracious rule of Compensation.

—Martin Farquhar Tupper
"Of Compensation." *Proverbial Philosophy: A Book of Thoughts and Arguments.*

Chapter 9

THE LAW OF RELATIVITY

The Law of Relativity maintains that experiences and circumstances occur in isolation in the physical world in relation to our mind and conscious awareness. It is our human perceptions of emotions, feelings, thoughts, and judgments about those experiences that colors them and labels them positive or negative in our consciousness. This law advises us that there are contrasting viewpoints and opinions that we can have on these experiences and life situations, and this can help us find and choose balanced and positive reactions. The individual can always decide how something will affect their mental state, their outlook, and their reaction.

This law contends that it is more beneficial to adjust our focus toward positive, productive thinking and away from negative, non-productive thinking to avail ourselves of the Law of Relativity. Practicing the virtues of patience, gratitude, humility, kindness, charity, courage, and duty can help an individual have this valuable focus.

Good and evil are thereby seen to be but relative terms indicating the result of our thoughts and actions. If we entertain constructive thoughts only, the result will benefit ourselves or others, this benefit we call good, if on the other hand we entertain destructive thought, this will result in inharmony for ourselves and others, this inharmony we call evil, but the power is the same in either event. There is but one source of power and we can use the power for good or for evil, just as we can make use of electricity for light, heat or power by an understanding of the laws governing electricity, but if we are careless or ignorant of the laws governing electricity, the result may be disastrous. The power is not good in one case and evil in the other; the good or evil depend upon our understanding of the law.

—Charles F. Haanel
Mental Chemistry.

Inasmuch as it teaches us, how we ought to conduct ourselves with respect to the gifts of fortune, or matters which are not in our power, and do not follow from our nature. For it shows us, that we should await and endure fortune's smiles or frowns with an equal mind, seeing that all things follow from the eternal decree of God by the same necessity, as it follows from the essence of a triangle, that the three angles are equal to two right angles.

—Benedict de Spinoza
The Ethics.

Plato compared human life to a game at dice, wherein we ought to throw according to our requirements, and, having thrown, to make the best use of whatever turns up. It is not in our power indeed to determine what the throw will be, but it is our part, if we are wise, to accept in a right spirit whatever fortune sends.

—Plutarch
"On Contentedness of Mind."

I built a chimney for a comrade old;
  I did the service not for hope of hire:
And then I travelled on in winter's cold
  Yet all the day I glowed before the fire.

—Edwin Markham
"Two at a Fireside." *The Man with the Hoe And Other Poems.*

Time, years, seasons, accordingly, are not to be esteemed a part of creation, but simply as an accident or result of it. Our personal experiences concur with nature in testifying to this, for to no two men has time the same duration, nor does any individual reckon it always by the same dial. To the slothful, time has the feet of a snail; to the diligent, the wings of an eagle. Impatience lengthens, enjoyment shortens it. The unhappy and desolate see nothing but weary tedium; with the cheerful it glides like a stream.

—Leo Hartley Grindon
"Time and Seasons." *Life: Its Nature, Varieties, and Phenomena.*

Let there be many windows to your soul,
That all the glory of the universe
May beautify it…………
And throw your soul wide open to the light
Of Reason and of knowledge. Tune your ear
To all the wordless music of the stars,
And to the voice of Nature; and your heart
Shall turn to truth and goodness as the plant
Turns to the sun. A thousand unseen hands
Reach down to help you to their peace-crowned heights,
And all the forces of the firmament
Shall fortify your strength. Be not afraid
To thrust aside half-truths and grasp the whole.

—Ella Wheeler Wilcox
"Progress." *Poems of Passion.*

We are escorted on every hand through life by spiritual agents, and a beneficent purpose lies in wait for us. We cannot bandy words with nature, or deal with her as we deal with persons. If we measure our individual forces against hers, we may easily feel as if we were the sport of an insuperable destiny. But if, instead of identifying ourselves with the work, we feel that the soul of the workman streams through us, we shall find the peace of the morning dwelling first in our hearts, and the fathomless powers of gravity and chemistry, and, over them, of life preexisting within us in their highest form.

—Ralph Waldo Emerson
Nature.

Cease, then, nor order imperfection name:
Our proper bliss depends on what we blame.
Know thy own point: this kind, this due degree
Of blindness, weakness, Heaven bestows on thee.
Submit. In this, or any other sphere,
Secure to be as blest as thou canst bear:
Safe in the hand of one disposing Power,
Or in the natal, or the mortal hour.
All nature is but art, unknown to thee;
All chance, direction, which thou canst not see;
All discord, harmony not understood;
All partial evil, universal good:
And, spite of pride in erring reason's spite,
One truth is clear, whatever is, is right.

—ALEXANDER POPE
An Essay on Man. Moral Essays and Satires.

"There is nothing either good or bad, but thinking makes it so."

– WILLIAM SHAKESPEARE
Hamlet.

So true is it that nothing is wretched, but thinking makes it so, and conversely every lot is happy if borne with equanimity.

—BOETHIUS
"IV, Book II." *The Consolation of Philosophy of Boethius.*

Who can dispute that a mind, which supports a perpetual serenity and cheerfulness, a noble dignity and undaunted spirit, a tender affection and goodwill to all around; as it has more enjoyment within itself, is also a more animating and rejoicing spectacle, than if dejected with melancholy, tormented with anxiety, irritated with rage……

—DAVID HUME
Essays Moral, Political, and Literary.

But surely, I deny not the course itself of events, which lies open to every one's inquiry and examination. I acknowledge, that, in the present order of things, virtue is attended with more peace of mind than vice, and meets with a more favourable reception from the world. I am sensible, that, according to the past experience of mankind, friendship is the chief joy of human life, and moderation the only source of tranquillity and happiness. I never balance between the virtuous and the vicious course of life; but am sensible, that, to a well-disposed mind, every advantage is on the side of the former.

—DAVID HUME
An Enquiry Concerning the Human Understanding, And An Enquiry Concerning the Principles of Morals.

One more trait of true success. The good mind chooses what is positive, what is advancing,—embraces the affirmative.

Omit the negative propositions. Nerve us with incessant affirmatives. Don't waste yourself in rejection, nor bark against the bad, but chant the beauty of the good. When that is spoken which has a right to be spoken, the chatter and the criticism will stop. Set down nothing that will not help somebody.

—Ralph Waldo Emerson
"Success." *Society and Solitude.*

The chief pang of most trials is not so much the actual suffering itself, as our own spirit of resistance to it. But a soul that accepts its own nothingness is free from this resistance, and nothing can disturb its peace – the habit of renunciation strengthens continually, and we are astonished to find ourselves bearing that which once seemed intolerable, calmly and patiently.

—Pere Jean Nicolas Grou
The Hidden Life of the Soul.

Yet hope itself a brightness throws
O'er all our labours and our woes;
While dark foreboding Care
A thousand ills will oft portend,
That Providence may ne'er intend
The trembling heart to bear.

Or if they come, it oft appears,
Our woes are lighter than our fears,
And far more bravely borne.
Then let us not enhance our doom;
But e'en in midnight's blackest gloom
Expect the rising morn.

Because the road is rough and long,
Shall we despise the skylark's song,
That cheers the wanderer's way?
Or trample down, with reckless feet,
The smiling flowerets, bright and sweet,
Because they soon decay?

Pass pleasant scenes unnoticed by,
Because the next is bleak and drear;
Or not enjoy a smiling sky,
Because a tempest may be near?

No! while we journey on our way,
We'll smile on every lovely thing;
And ever, as they pass away,
To memory and hope we'll cling.

—Anne Brontë
"Views of Life." *Poems by Currer, Ellis, and Acton Bell.*
(Charlotte Brontë, Emily Brontë and Anne Brontë).

Peace does not dwell in outward things, but within the soul. We may preserve it in the midst of the bitterest pain, if our will remains firm and submissive. Peace in this life springs from acquiescence even in disagreeable things, not in an exemption from bearing them.

—Francois de Salignac de La Mothe Fénelon
Selections from Fénelon.

But thou, want not! ask not! Find full reward
Of doing right in right! Let right deeds be
Thy motive, not the fruit which comes from them.
And live in action! Labour! Make thine acts
Thy piety, casting all self aside,
Contemning gain and merit; equable
In good or evil: equability
Is Yog, is piety!

—The Bhagavad-Gita.

As for myself, "I was bred to the plow." Amid the rugged hills, along the banks of Green River in Kentucky, I enjoyed the inestimable blessings of cabin life and hard work during the whole of my early days. I was in bondage, — I never was a slave,— the infamous laws of a savage despotism took my substance—what of that? Many a man has lost all he had, excepting his manhood. Adversity is the school of heroism, endurance the majesty of man and hope the torch of high aspirations. Acquainted with adversity, I am flattered of hope and comforted by endurance.

—Albery Allson Whitman
"Dedicatory Address." *The Rape of Florida.*

O while I live to be the ruler of life, not a slave,
To meet life as a powerful conqueror,
No fumes, no ennui, no more complaints or scornful criticisms,
To these proud laws of the air, the water and the ground, proving my interior soul impregnable,
And nothing exterior shall ever take command of me.

—Walt Whitman
"Song of Joys." *Leaves of Grass.*

And so, after living more than four score years in the world, and pondering long and intently upon the many problems which life and nature present, I have come, like Margaret Fuller, to accept the universe, have come frankly to accept that first verdict pronounced upon creation, namely, that it is very good — good in its sum total up to this astronomic date, whatever phases it may at times present that lead us to a contrary conclusion.

Not that cold and hunger, war and pestilence, tornadoes and earthquakes, are good in a positive sense, but that these and kindred things are vastly overbalanced by the forces and agencies that make for our well-being, — that "work together for good," — the sunshine, the cooling breezes, the fertile soil, the stability of land and sea, the gentle currents, the equipoise of the forces of the earth, air, and water, the order and security of our solar system, and, in the human realm, the good-will and fellowship that are finally bound to prevail among men and nations.

—John Burroughs
"Shall We Accept the Universe?" *Accepting the Universe. Essays in Naturalism.*

Well, thou knowest the will of nature. Will then this which has happened prevent thee from being just, magnanimous, temperate, prudent, secure against inconsiderate opinions and falsehood; will it prevent thee from having modesty, freedom, and everything else, by the presence of which man's nature obtains all that is its own? Remember too on every occasion which leads thee to vexation to apply this principle; not that this is a misfortune, but that to bear it nobly is good fortune.

—Marcus Aurelius
The Meditations of Marcus Aurelius.

It is in our power to have no opinion about a thing, and not to be disturbed in our soul; for things themselves have no natural power to form our judgments.

Everywhere and at all times it is in thy power piously to acquiesce in thy present condition, and to behave, justly to those who are about thee, and to exert thy skill upon thy present thoughts, that nothing shall steal into them without being well examined.

—Marcus Aurelius
The Meditations of Marcus Aurelius.

Not that I speak in respect of want: for I have learned, in whatsoever state I am, therewith to be content.

—Philippians 4:11. *KJV.*

If thou art pained by any external thing, it is not this thing that disturbs thee, but thy own judgment about it. And it is in thy power to wipe out this judgment now. But if anything in thy own disposition gives thee pain, who hinders thee from correcting thy opinion? And even if thou art pained because thou art not doing some particular thing which seems to thee to be right, why dost thou not rather act than complain?

—Marcus Aurelius
The Meditations of Marcus Aurelius.

Everything has two handles, the one by which it may be borne, the other by which it may not. If your brother acts unjustly, do not lay hold of the act by that handle wherein he acts unjustly, for this is the handle which cannot be borne; but lay hold of the other, that he is your brother, that he was nurtured with you, and you will lay hold of the thing by that handle by which it can be borne.

—Epictetus
"XLIII." *The Encheiridion, or Manual.*

My neighbor likes the lowing of his herds;
To shut it out I draw my window down,
And read my latest volume from the town;
My poem to my neighbor is but words;

My neighbor's feast to me is whey and curds;
His hands applaud the tinselled circus clown,
In Wagner's genius I my senses drown,

And each his life with fitting cincture girds.

Thus neighbored, yet so very far asunder,
Contentedly we take divided ways;
Why should I term his stature lack of growth?

He does not ask my lightning for his thunder,
I do not take my measure by his praise,
And so the world is wide enough for both.

—Mary Ashley Townsend
"XVIII." *Distaff and Spindle: Sonnets.*

The Buddha's teaching, Adapting oneself to circumstances, and our Confucian precept, Doing what is due to one's situation, rich or poor, — these sayings are the life-buoys indispensable for navigating the rough sea of life. Boundless are the paths of human existence; in our journey along them, we are bound to meet with numberless rubs and obstacles. If we long for perfection, we shall be annoyed with a thousand worries. On the contrary, if we are contented with our lot, there is not any position in society but gives us peace of mind.

—Hung Ying-Ming
Musings of a Chinese Vegetarian.

Let us as individuals banish the word "Hurry" from our lives. Let us care for nothing so much that we would pay honor and self-respect as the price of hurrying it. Let us cultivate calmness, restfulness, poise, sweetness, — doing our best, bearing all things as bravely as we can; living our life undisturbed by the prosperity of the wicked or the malice of the envious. Let us not be impatient, chafing at delay, fretting over failure, wearying over results, and weakening under opposition. Let us ever turn our face toward the future with confidence and trust, with the calmness of a life in harmony with itself, true to its ideals, and slowly and constantly progressing toward their realization.

—William George Jordan
The Majesty of Calmness.

Some murmur, when their sky is clear
And wholly bright to view,
If one small speck of dark appear
In their great heaven of blue.
And some with thankful love are filled
If but one streak of light,
One ray of God's good mercy gild
The darkness of their night.
In palaces are hearts that ask,
In discontent and pride,
Why life is such a dreary task,
And all good things denied.
And hearts in poorest huts admire
How love has in their aid
(Love that not ever seems to tire)
Such rich provision made.

—Richard Chenevix Trench
"Some Murmur, When Their Sky is Clear."
Sabbation; Honor Neale; and Other Poems.

Seek not that the things which happen should happen as you wish; but wish the things which happen to be as they are, and you will have a tranquil flow of life.

—Epictetus
"VIII." *The Encheiridion, or Manual.*

The knower and the ignorant are both equally subject each to his own previous Karma; — the knower, all patience, knows no sorrow; the ignorant, ever unsteady, continues to grieve. Of two men passing on the road, both being equally fatigued and the road before them being equal, he that knows treads on patiently to the end, the poor ignorant fool lingers behind bemoaning his lot.

—Panchadasi
("Liberation." *The Spirit of the Upanishads; Or, The Aphorisms of the Wise.*)

It seems to me reasonable to enjoy blessings with confidence, as well as to resign them with submission, and to hope for the continuance of good which we possess without insolence or voluptuousness, as for the restitution of that which we lose without despondency or murmurs.

The chief security against the fruitless anguish of impatience, must arise from frequent reflection on the wisdom and goodness of the God of nature, in whose hands are riches and poverty, honour and disgrace, pleasure and pain, and life and death. A settled conviction of the tendency of every thing to our good, and of the possibility of turning miseries into happiness, by receiving them rightly, will incline us to bless the name of the Lord, whether he gives or takes away.

—Samuel Johnson
"No. 32." *The Rambler. Vol. 1.*
(*The Works of Samuel Johnson*).

Black as the Pit from pole to pole,
I thank whatever gods may be
For my unconquerable soul.
In the fell clutch of circumstance
I have not winced nor cried aloud.
Under the bludgeonings of chance
My head is bloody, but unbowed.
Beyond this place of wrath and tears
Looms but the Horror of the shade,
And yet the menace of the years
Finds, and shall find, me unafraid.
It matters not how strait the gate,
How charged with punishments the scroll.
I am the master of my fate:
I am the captain of my soul.

—William Ernest Henley
"Invictus."

We refuse to be unduly depressed in the gloom, as we refused to be unduly elated in the light; we balance one experience against the other, removing the thorn of present pain by the memory of past joy and the foretaste of joy in the future; we learn in happiness to remember sorrow and in sorrow to remember happiness, till neither the one nor the other can shake the steady foothold of the soul. Thus we begin to rise above the lower stages of consciousness in which we are flung from one extreme to the other, and to gain the equilibrium which is called yoga. Thus the existence of the law becomes to us not a theory but a conviction, and we gradually learn something of the peace of the Self.

—ANNIE BESANT
"Some Difficulties of the Inner Life."
Some Problems of Life.

COUNT each affliction, whether light or grave,
God's messenger sent down to thee; do thou
With courtesy receive him; rise and bow;
Then lay before him all thou hast; allow
No cloud of passion to usurp thy brow,
Or mar thy hospitality; no wave
Of mortal tumult to obliterate
The soul's marmoreal calmness: Grief should be,
Like joy, majestic, equable, sedate;
Confirming, cleansing, raising, making free;
Strong to consume small troubles; to commend
Great thoughts, grave thoughts, thoughts lasting to the end.

—AUBREY DE VERE
"Sorrow."

Who are the Wise?
They who have governed with a self-controul,
Each wild and baneful passion of the soul;

Curbed the strong impulse of all fierce desires,
But kept alive affection's purer fires;
They who have passed the labyrinth of life,
Without one hour of weakness or of strife;
Prepared each change of fortune to endure,
Humble though rich, and dignified though poor;
Skilled in the latent movements of the heart—
Learned in that lore which Nature can impart;
Teaching that sweet philosophy aloud,
Which sees the "silver lining" of the cloud;
Looking for good in all beneath the skies: —
These are the truly Wise!

—John Critchley Prince.
"Who Are the Free!" *Hours with the Muses.*

I would not ask Thee that my days
Should flow quite smoothly on and on,
Lest I should learn to love the world
Too well, ere all my time was done.

But I would ask a humble heart,
A changeless will to work and wake,
A firm faith in Thy providence,
The rest—'tis thine to give or take.

—Alfred Norris
"A Prayer." *Inner and Outer Life: Poems.*

As to living in the best way, this power is in the soul, if it be indifferent to things which are indifferent. And it will be indifferent, if it looks on each of these things separately and all together, and if it remembers that not one of them produces in us an opinion about itself, nor comes to us; but these things remain immovable, and it is we ourselves who produce the judgments about them, and, as we may say, write them in ourselves, it being in our power not to write them, and it being in our power, if perchance these judgments have imperceptibly got admission to our minds, to wipe them out…

—Marcus Aurelius
The Meditations of Marcus Aurelius.

Let man, then, submit to necessity: in despite of himself it will always hurry him forward: let him resign himself to Nature, let him accept the good with which she presents him: let him oppose to the necessary evil which she makes him experience, those necessary remedies which she consents to afford him; let him not disturb his mind with useless inquietude; let him enjoy with moderation, because he will find that pain is the necessary companion of excess: let him follow the paths of virtue, because every thing will prove to him, even in this world of perverseness, that it is absolutely necessary to render him estimable in the eyes of others, to make him contented with himself.

—Baron d'Holbach (Paul-Henri Thiry)
"Chapter XII." *The System of Nature, Or, Laws of the Moral and Physical World.*

Chapter 10

THE LAW OF POLARITY

The Law of Polarity states that everything is dual in nature. This dualism maintains that each thing has an opposite necessary for balance in our universe. These complimentary opposites are not separate things, but inseparable parts that create a whole; they become two parts of the same thing.

This Law of Polarity is exhibited in our human experience in a variety of related ways. It is seen in the kindred concepts of balance, harmony, contrast, moderation, the golden mean, the Yin/Yang of Taoism, the Middle Way of Buddhism, and in the Law of Gender. This dual nature of reality is an essential aspect of the physical world and our inner mental world.

That great principle of Undulation in nature, that shows itself in the inspiring and expiring of the breath; in desire and satiety; in the ebb and flow of the sea; in day and night; in heat and cold; and, as yet more deeply ingrained in every atom and every fluid, is known to us under the name of Polarity,— these "fits of easy transmission and reflection," as Newton called them, are the law of nature because they are the law of spirit.

—RALPH WALDO EMERSON
"The American Scholar."

True observers of nature, although they may think differently, will still agree that everything that is, everything that is observable as a phenomenon, can only exhibit itself in one of two ways. It is either a primal polarity that is able to unify, or it is a primal unity that is able to divide. To divide the united, and unite the divided, is the life of nature; this is the eternal systole and diastole, the eternal collapsion and expansion, the inspiration and expiration of the world in which we live and move.

—Johann Wolfgang von Goethe
"Relation to General Physics."
Goethe's Theory of Colours.

Polarity, or action and reaction, we meet in every part of nature; in darkness and light; in heat and cold; in the ebb and flow of waters; in male and female; in the inspiration and expiration of plants and animals; in the equation of quantity and quality in the fluids of the animal body; in the systole and diastole of the heart; in the undulations of fluids, and of sound; in the centrifugal and centripetal gravity; in electricity, galvanism, and chemical affinity. Superinduce magnetism at one end of a needle; the opposite magnetism takes place at the other end. If the south attracts, the north repels. To empty here, you must condense there. An inevitable dualism bisects nature, so that each thing is a half, and suggests another thing to make it whole; as, spirit, matter; man, woman; odd, even; subjective, objective; in, out; upper, under; motion, rest; yea, nay. Whilst the world is thus dual, so is every one of its parts. The entire system of things gets represented in every particle. There is somewhat that resembles the ebb and flow of the sea, day and night, man and woman, in a single needle of the pine, in a kernel of corn, in each individual of every animal tribe. The reaction, so grand in the elements, is repeated within these small boundaries.

....

The same dualism underlies the nature and condition of man. Every excess causes a defect; every defect an excess. Every sweet hath its sour; every evil its good. Every faculty which is a receiver of pleasure has an equal penalty put on its abuse. It is to answer for its moderation with its life. For every grain of wit there is a grain of folly. For everything you have missed, you have gained something else; and for everything you gain, you lose something. If riches increase, they are increased that use them. If the gatherer gathers too much, nature takes out of the man what she puts into his chest, swells the estate, but kills the owner. Nature hates monopolies and exceptions. The waves of the sea do not more speedily seek a level from their loftiest tossing, than the varieties of condition tend to equalize themselves. There is always some leveling circumstance that puts down the overbearing, the strong, the rich, the fortunate, substantially on the same ground with all others.

—RALPH WALDO EMERSON
"Compensation." *Essays, First Series.*

"Everything is Dual; everything has poles; everything has its pair of opposites; like and unlike are the same; opposites are identical in nature, but different in degree; extremes meet; all truths are but half-truths; all paradoxes may be reconciled."

—"The Seven Hermetic Principles."
The Kybalion.

In psychological reflection the greatest difficulty is this: that inner and outer must always be viewed in parallel lines, or, rather, interwoven. It is a continual systole and diastole, an inspiration and an expiration of the living soul. If this cannot be put into words, it should be carefully marked and noted.

—Johann Wolfgang Von Goethe
"Literature and Art." The Maxims and
Reflections of Goethe.

Being and non-being produce each other.
Difficult and easy complement each other.
Long and short define each other.
High and low oppose each other.
Fore and aft follow each other.

—Lao-Tzu
Tao Te Ching.

The danger that threatens repose is stagnation, that threatens industry is greed, that threatens thrift is avarice, that threatens power is tyranny. Everywhere are things linked together, every virtue has its vice, every good has its ill, every sweet has its bitter, and the bitter is often the best medicine.

—John Burroughs
"All's Right With The World." *Leaf and Tendril.*

Heraclitus called discord and concord the universal parents. And to rail at discord (says the father of the poets) is to speak ill of nature.

It is vicissitude that maintains the world.

Surely we deceive ourselves, to think that continued joys would please: this is against the order of nature.

Crosses and ills are sometimes the better part of our life: I know not well which is the more useful. Joy I may choose for pleasure; but adversities are the best for profit; and sometimes these do so far help me, that without them, I should want much of the joy I have.

—Owen Felltham
*Resolve, Divine, Moral and Political
of Owen Felltham.*

Two principles in human nature reign;
Self-love, to urge, and reason, to restrain;
Nor this a good, nor that a bad we call,
Each works its end, to move or govern all:
And to their proper operation still,
Ascribe all good; to their improper, ill.

Self-love, the spring of motion, acts the soul;
Reason's comparing balance rules the whole.
Man, but for that, no action could attend,
And but for this, were active to no end:
Fix'd like a plant on his peculiar spot,
To draw nutrition, propagate, and rot;
Or, meteor-like, flame lawless through the void,
Destroying others, by himself destroy'd.

Most strength the moving principle requires;
Active its task, it prompts, impels, inspires.
Sedate and quiet the comparing lies,
Form'd but to check, delib'rate, and advise.
Self-love still stronger, as its objects nigh;
Reason's at distance, and in prospect lie:
That sees immediate good by present sense;
Reason, the future and the consequence.
Thicker than arguments, temptations throng,
At best more watchful this, but that more strong.
The action of the stronger to suspend,
Reason still use, to reason still attend.
Attention, habit and experience gains;
Each strengthens reason, and self-love restrains.

Let subtle schoolmen teach these friends to fight,
More studious to divide than to unite,
And grace and virtue, sense and reason split,
With all the rash dexterity of wit:
Wits, just like fools, at war about a name,
Have full as oft no meaning, or the same.
Self-love and reason to one end aspire,
Pain their aversion, pleasure their desire;
But greedy that its object would devour,

This taste the honey, and not wound the flow'r:
Pleasure, or wrong or rightly understood,
Our greatest evil, or our greatest good.

—ALEXANDER POPE
An Essay on Man. *Moral Essays and Satires.*

The passions of mankind are partly protective, partly beneficent, like the chaff and grain of the corn; but none without their use, none without nobleness when seen in balanced unity with the rest of the spirit which they are charged to defend.

—JOHN RUSKIN
"The Nature of Gothic." *Stones of Venice, Vol. 2*

And the priestess spoke again and said: Speak to us of Reason and Passion.
And he answered, saying:
Your soul is oftentimes a battlefield, upon which your reason and your judgment wage war against your passion and your appetite.
Would that I could be the peacemaker in your soul, that I might turn the discord and the rivalry of your elements into oneness and melody.
But how shall I, unless you yourselves be also the peacemakers, nay, the lovers of all your elements?
Your reason and your passion are the rudder and the sails of your seafaring soul.
If either your sails or your rudder be broken, you can but toss and drift, or else be held at a standstill in mid-seas.

For reason, ruling alone, is a force confining; and passion, unattended, is a flame that burns to its own destruction.
Therefore let your soul exalt your reason to the height of passion, that it may sing;
And let it direct your passion with reason, that your passion may live through its own daily resurrection, and like the phoenix rise above its own ashes.
I would have you consider your judgment and your appetite even as you would two loved guests in your house.
Surely you would not honour one guest above the other; for he who is more mindful of one loses the love and the faith of both.
Among the hills, when you sit in the cool shade of the white poplars, sharing the peace and serenity of distant fields and meadows—then let your heart say in silence, "God rests in reason."
And when the storm comes, and the mighty wind shakes the forest, and thunder and lightning proclaim the majesty of the sky,—then let your heart say in awe, "God moves in passion."
And since you are a breath in God's sphere, and a leaf in God's forest, you too should rest in reason and move in passion.

—KAHLIL GIBRAN
The Prophet.

Thought without action is an evil, and so is action without thought. The ideal is a poison unless it be fused with the real, and the real becomes corrupt without the perfume of the ideal. Nothing is good singly without its complement and its contrary.

Self-examination is dangerous if it encroaches upon self-devotion; reverie is hurtful when it stupefies the will; gentleness is an evil when it lessens strength; contemplation is fatal when it destroys character. "Too much" and "too little" sin equally against wisdom. Excess is one evil, apathy another. Duty may be defined as energy tempered by moderation; happiness, as inclination calmed and tempered by self-control.

—Henri-Frédéric Amiel
Amiel's Journal: The Journal Intime of Henri-Frédéric Amiel.

In childhood's pride I said to Thee:
"O Thou, who mad'st me of Thy breath,
Speak, Master, and reveal to me
Thine inmost laws of life and death.

"Give me to drink each joy and pain
Which Thine eternal hand can mete,
For my insatiate soul would drain
Earth's utmost bitter, utmost sweet.

"Spare me no bliss, no pang of strife,
Withhold no gift or grief I crave,
The intricate lore of love and life
And mystic knowledge of the grave."

Lord, Thou didst answer stern and low:
"Child, I will hearken to thy prayer,
And thy unconquered soul shall know
All passionate rapture and despair.

"Thou shalt drink deep of joy and fame,
And love shall burn thee like a fire,
And pain shall cleanse thee like a flame,
To purge the dross from thy desire.

"So shall thy chastened spirit yearn
To seek from its blind prayer release,
And spent and pardoned, sue to learn
The simple secret of My peace.

"I, bending from my sevenfold height
Will teach thee of My quickening grace,
Life is a prism of My light,
And Death the shadow of My face."

—Sarojini Naidu
"The Soul's Prayer." *The Bird of Time. Songs of Life, Death & the Spring.*

And yet 'tis just the golden mean
That checks our lives' unsteady flow;
God's counterbalance thrown between,
To poise the scale 'twixt joy and woe:
And better so; for were the bowl
Too freely to the parched lip given,
Too much of grief would crush the soul,
Too much of joy would wean from heaven.

—Egbert Phelps
"Life's Incongruities."

In the day of prosperity be joyful, but in the day of adversity consider: God also hath set the one over against the other, to the end that man should find nothing after him.

—Ecclesiastes 7:14. *KJV.*

IT WAS an high speech of Seneca (after the manner of the Stoics), that the good things, which belong to prosperity, are to be wished; but the good things, that belong to adversity, are to be admired……

But to speak in a mean. The virtue of prosperity, is temperance; the virtue of adversity, is fortitude; which in morals is the more heroical virtue. Prosperity is the blessing of the Old Testament; adversity is the blessing of the New; which carrieth the greater benediction, and the clearer revelation of God's favor………..

Prosperity is not without many fears and distastes; and adversity is not without comforts and hopes. We see in needle-works and embroideries, it is more pleasing to have a lively work, upon a sad and solemn ground, than to have a dark and melancholy work, upon a lightsome ground: judge therefore of the pleasure of the heart, by the pleasure of the eye. Certainly virtue is like precious odors, most fragrant when they are incensed, or crushed: for prosperity doth best discover vice, but adversity doth best discover virtue.

—Francis Bacon
"Adversity." *Essays or Counsels Civil and Moral.*
The Works of Francis Bacon.

All virtues lie between
Excess and defect,
A narrow path betwixt
Hell's bottomless abyss,
Fine and sharp as a sword blade,
Which permits no lingering
Or turning round.
Equipoise is the summit of perfection,
Becoming like a simple essence.
As the rays of the sun
Shine upon the earth,
So the Light from the Spirit World
Shines brightly on him
Who has attained this equilibrium.

—MAHMUD SHABISTARI
The Secret Rose Garden of Sa'd Ud Din Mahmud Shabistari.

Good and ill seems as necessary to human life as light and shade are to a picture. We grow weary of uniform success, and pleasure soon surfeits. Pain makes ease delightful; hunger relishes the homeliest food, fatigue turns the hardest bed to down; and the difficulty and uncertainty of pursuits in all cases enhanced the value of possession.

—WILLIAM HAZLITT
"CCLXXXVII." *Characteristics: in the manner of Rochefoucault's Maxims.*

Good and ill are universally intermingled and confounded; happiness and misery, wisdom and folly, virtue and vice. Nothing is pure and entirely of a piece. All advantages are attended with disadvantages. An universal compensation prevails in all conditions of being and existence.

The more exquisite any good is, of which a small specimen is afforded us, the sharper is the evil allied to it; and few exceptions are found to this uniform law of nature.

—David Hume
Essays Moral, Political, and Literary.

But, as we use our brightest colours in a picture, so in the mind we ought to look at the cheerful and bright side of things, and hide and keep down the gloomy, for we cannot altogether obliterate or get rid of it. For, as the strings of the bow and lyre are alternately tightened and relaxed, so is it with the order of the world; in human affairs there is nothing pure and without alloy. But as in music there are high and low notes, and in grammar vowels and mutes, but neither the musician nor grammarian decline to use either kinds, but know how to blend and employ them both for their purpose, so in human affairs which are balanced one against another,-for, as Euripides says, "There is no good without ill in the world, but everything is mixed in due proportion,"-we ought not to be disheartened or despondent; but as musicians drown their worst music with the best, so should we take good and bad together, and make our chequered life one of convenience and harmony.

—Plutarch
"On Contentedness of Mind." *Plutarch's Morals: Ethical Essays.*

Everything in nature is bipolar, or has a positive and negative pole. There is a male and a female, a spirit and a fact, a north and a south. Spirit is the positive, the event is the negative. Will is the north, action the south pole. Character may be ranked as having its natural place in the north. It shares the magnetic currents of the system. The feeble souls are drawn to the south or negative pole. They look at the profit or hurt of the action. They never behold a principle until it is lodged in a person.

—Ralph Waldo Emerson
"Character." Essays, Second Series.

For hope and fear, how distant soever they may seem to be the one from the other, they are both of them yet coupled in the same chain, as the guard and the prisoner; and the one treads upon the heels of the other. The reason of this is obvious, for they are passions that look forward, and are ever solicitous for the future; only hope is the more plausible weakness of the two, which in truth, upon the main, are inseparable; for the one cannot be without the other: but where the hope is stronger than the fear, or the fear than the hope, we call it the one or the other; for without fear it were no longer hope, but certainty; as without hope it were no longer fear but despair.

—Lucius Annaeus Seneca
"Of a Happy Life."

Suffering is doubtless as divinely appointed as joy, while it is much more influential as a discipline of character. It chastens and sweetens the nature, teaches patience and resignation, and promotes the deepest as well as the most exalted thought.

Suffering may be the appointed means by which the highest nature of man is to be disciplined and developed. Assuming happiness to be the end of being, sorrow may be the indispensable condition through which it is to be reached.

Life, all sunshine without shade, all happiness without sorrow, all pleasure without pain, were not life at all—at least not human life. Take the lot of the happiest—it is a tangled yarn. It is made up of sorrows and joys; and the joys are all the sweeter because of the sorrows; bereavements and blessings, one following another, making us sad and blessed by turns.

—Samuel Smiles
"Chapter XII. The Discipline of Experience." *Character*.

We must learn to suffer what we cannot evade; our life, like the harmony of the world, is composed of contrary things—of diverse tones, sweet and harsh, sharp and flat, sprightly and solemn: the musician who should only affect some of these, what would he be able to do? he must know how to make use of them all, and to mix them; and so we should mingle the goods and evils which are consubstantial with our life; our being cannot subsist without this mixture, and the one part is no less necessary to it than the other.

—Michel de Montaigne
"Chapter XIII. Of Experience. Book III." *The Essays of Michel de Montaigne*.

It is right it should be so;
Man was made for joy and woe;
And when this we rightly know,
Thro' the world we safely go.
Joy and woe are woven fine,
A clothing for the soul divine.
Under every grief and pine
Runs a joy with silken twine.

—William Blake
"Auguries of Innocence."

O to share the great, sunny, joyous life of the earth! to be as happy as the birds are! as contented as the cattle on the hills! as the leaves of the trees that dance and rustle in the wind! as the waters that murmur and sparkle to the sea! 'To be able to see that the sin and sorrow and suffering of the world are a necessary part of the natural course of things, a phase of the law of growth and development that runs through the universe, bitter in its personal application, but illuminating when we look upon life as a whole! Without death and decay, how could life go on? Without what we call sin (which is another name for imperfection) and the struggle consequent upon it, how could our development proceed?

—John Burroughs
"An Outlook Upon Life." *Leaf and Tendril.*

When you are joyous, look deep into your heart and you shall find it is only that which has given you sorrow that is giving you joy.

When you are sorrowful look again in your heart, and you shall see that in truth you are weeping for that which has been your delight.
Some of you say, "Joy is greater than sorrow," and others say, "Nay, sorrow is the greater."
But I say unto you, they are inseparable.
Together they come, and when one sits alone with you at your board, remember that the other is asleep upon your bed.
Verily you are suspended like scales between your sorrow and your joy.

—Kahlil Gibran
The Prophet.

Neither joy nor sorrow; neither movable nor immovably fixed; neither being nor non-being; nay not even the intermediate between these opposites -so is described the mind of the enlightened.

—*Yogavasishtha*
"Liberation." *The Spirit of the Upanishads; Or, The Aphorisms of the Wise.*

Let no man pray that he know not sorrow,
Let no soul ask to be free from pain,
For the gall of to-day is the sweet of to-morrow,
And the moment's loss is the lifetime's gain.
Through want of a thing does its worth redouble,
Through hunger's pangs does the feast content,
And only the heart that has harbored trouble,
Can fully rejoice when joy is sent.

Let no man shrink from the bitter tonics
Of grief, and yearning, and need, and strife,
For the rarest chords in the soul's harmonies,
Are found in the minor strains of life.

—Ella Wheeler Wilcox
"Life's Harmonies". *Poems of Power*

I enjoin my soul to look upon pain and pleasure with an eye equally regular, and equally firm; but the one gaily and the other severely, and so far as it is able, to be careful to extinguish the one as to extend the other. The judging rightly of good brings along with it the judging soundly of evil: pain has something of the inevitable in its tender beginnings, and pleasure something of the evitable in its excessive end. Plato couples them together, and wills that it should be equally the office of fortitude to fight against pain, and against the immoderate and charming blandishments of pleasure: they are two fountains, from which whoever draws, when and as much as he needs, whether city, man, or beast, is very fortunate. The first is to be taken medicinally and upon necessity, and more scantily; the other for thirst, but not to, drunkenness. Pain, pleasure, love and hatred are the first things that a child is sensible of: if, when reason comes, they apply it to themselves, that is virtue.

—Michel de Montaigne
"Chapter XIII. Of Experience. Book III." *The Essays of Michel de Montaigne.*

Standing alone, in vale or mountain-top,
Upon the grassy plain, or ocean shore,
Or far away upon a ship at sea,
We are the middle of the Universe.
Around us as a centre, Earth and Heaven
Describe their mystic circles evermore.
We move; and all the radii shape themselves
To the one point and focus of our eyes.

But in our mental life we disobey
The law of circles: on the outer verge
We stand for ever, sometimes looking down
Upon extraneous evil far removed
Beyond the bound of Earth's circumference,
Adown dark tangents, infinitely stretched,
Through gloomy Chaos, troubled by Despair.

At other times we seek the sunniest verge,
The amber and the purple blooms of Heaven,
And strive with yearning eyes, made dim by tears,
To pierce the secrets of a happier state.
Exulting are we now, - and now forlorn.

Lord grant us wisdom! grant that we may stand
In the fair middle of the spiritual world,
Undarken'd by the glooms of utter night,
Undazzled by the noontide glow of day.
True wisdom and serenity of soul
Dwell in the centre, and avoid extremes.

—Charles Mackay
"Serenity." *Voices from the Mountains and from the Crowd.*

Still, where rosy Pleasure leads,
See a kindred Grief pursue;
Behind the steps that Misery treads,
Approaching Comfort view:
The hues of bliss more brightly glow,
Chastis'd by sabler tints of woe;
And blended form, with artful strife,
The strength and harmony of life.

—Thomas Gray
"Ode on the Pleasure Arising from Vicissitude."

Chapter 11

The Law of Rhythm

The Law of Rhythm (also sometimes called the Law of Motion) states that the energies in the universe are cyclical, whether those energies manifest in the outer world of nature and our bodies, or the inner world of mind and spirit. Everything has cycles that are a natural part of the universe that constitute the ebbs and flows between different extremes.

The Law of Rhythm, or of periodicity, is evident throughout nature. This principle is seen in the tides of the oceans and the changing of the seasons, in the biorhythms of living things, in the movements of celestial bodies, in the regular, repeated patterns in music, in the ebb and flow of human feelings and emotions.

Everything flows out and in; everything has its tides; all things rise and fall; the pendulum-swing manifests in everything; the measure of the swing to the right, is the measure of the swing to the left; rhythm compensates.

—"The Seven Hermetic Principles."
The Kybalion.

There is something magical in rhythm; it even makes us believe that we possess the sublime.

        —Johann Wolfgang Von Goethe
      "131." *The Maxims and Reflections of Goethe.*

O! the one Life within us and abroad,
Which meets all motion and becomes its soul,
A light in sound, a sound-like power in light,
Rhythm in all thought, and joyance everywhere—
Methinks, it should have been impossible
Not to love all things in a world so filled;
Where the breeze warbles, and the mute still air
Is Music slumbering on her instrument.

Full many a thought uncalled and undetained,
And many idle flitting phantasies,
Traverse my indolent and passive brain,
As wild and various as the random gales
That swell and flutter on this subject Lute!

And what if all of animated nature
Be but organic Harps diversely framed,
That tremble into thought, as o'er them sweeps
Plastic and vast, one intellectual breeze,
At once the Soul of each, and God of all?

        —Samuel Taylor Coleridge
          "The Eolian Harp."

The sun also ariseth, and the sun goeth down, and hasteth to his place where he arose.

The wind goeth toward the south, and turneth about unto the north; it whirleth about continually, and the wind returneth again according to his circuits.

All the rivers run into the sea; yet the sea is not full; unto the place from whence the rivers come, thither they return again.

All things are full of labour; man cannot utter it: the eye is not satisfied with seeing, nor the ear filled with hearing.

The thing that hath been, it is that which shall be; and that which is done is that which shall be done: and there is no new thing under the sun.

Is there any thing whereof it may be said, See, this is new? it hath been already of old time, which was before us.

—Ecclesiastes 1: 5-10. *KJV.*

These alternations of happiness and depression are primarily manifestations of that law of periodicity, or law of rhythm, which guides the universe. Night and day alternate in the physical life of man as do happiness and depression in his emotional life. As the ebb and flow in the ocean, so are the ebb and flow in human feelings. There are tides in the human heart as in the affairs of men and as in the sea. Joy follows sorrow and sorrow follows joy, as surely as death follows birth and birth death. That this is so is not only a theory of a law, but it is also a fact to which witness is borne by all who have gained experience in the spiritual life.

—Annie Besant
"Some Difficulties of the Inner Life."
Some Problems of Life.

Day follows upon night, evening succeeds morning, the blast of withering cold follows the season full of flowers, and this over and over again. Time plays with the life of beings thus wearing out; and yet the whirl of Desire does never subside.

—S'ANKARACHARYA
"The Four-Fold Means." *The Spirit of the Upanishads; Or, The Aphorisms of the Wise.*

When auburn Autumn mounts the stage,
And Summer fails her charms to yield,
Bleak nature turns another page,
To light the glories of the field.
At once the vale declines to bloom,
The forest smiles no longer gay;
Gardens are left without perfume,
The rose and lilly pine away.
The orchard bows her fruitless head,
As one divested of her store;
Or like a queen whose train has fled,
And left her sad to smile no more.
That bird which breath'd her vernal song,
And hopp'd along the flow'ry spray,
Now silent holds her warbling tongue,
Which dulcifies the feast of May.
But let each bitter have its sweet,
No change of nature is in vain;
'Tis just alternate cold and heat,
For time is pleasure mix'd with pain.

—GEORGE MOSES HORTON
"Departing Summer."

If life is not always poetical, it is at least metrical. Periodicity rules over the mental experience of man, according to the path of the orbit of his thoughts. Distances are not gauged, ellipses not measured, velocities not ascertained, times not known. Nevertheless, the recurrence is sure. What the mind suffered last week, or last year, it does not suffer now; but it will suffer again next week or next year. Happiness is not a matter of events; it depends upon the tides of the mind.

Life seems so long, and its capacity so great, to one who knows nothing of all the intervals it needs must hold—intervals between aspirations, between actions, pauses as inevitable as the pauses of sleep. And life looks impossible to the young unfortunate, unaware of the inevitable and unfailing refreshment. It would be for their peace to learn that there is a tide in the affairs of men, in a sense more subtle—if it is not too audacious to add a meaning to Shakespeare—than the phrase was meant to contain. Their joy is flying away from them on its way home; their life will wax and wane; and if they would be wise, they must wake and rest in its phases, knowing that they are ruled by the law that commands all things.

—ALICE MEYNELL
"The Rhythm of Life." *The Rhythm of Life And Other Essays.*

So the year in spring's mild hours
Loads the air with scent of flowers;
Summer paints the golden grain
Then, when autumn comes again,
Bright with fruit the orchards glow;

Winter brings the rain and snow.
Thus the seasons' fixed progression,
Tempered in a due succession,
Nourishes and brings to birth
All that lives and breathes on earth.
Then, soon run life's little day,
All it brought it takes away.
But One sits and guides the reins,
He who made and all sustains;
King and Lord and Fountain-head,
Judge most holy, Law most dread;
Now impels and now keeps back,
Holds each waverer in the track.
Else, were once the power withheld
That the circling spheres compelled
In their orbits to revolve,
This world's order would dissolve,
And th' harmonious whole would all
In one hideous ruin fall.
But through this connected frame
Runs one universal aim;
Towards the Good do all things tend,
Many paths, but one the end.
For naught lasts, unless it turns
Backward in its course, and yearns
To that Source to flow again
Whence its being first was ta'en.

—Boethius
"Song VI, Book IV." *The Consolation of Philosophy of Boethius.*

Joy and anger, sorrow and happiness, caution and remorse, come upon us by turns, with ever-changing mood. They come like music from hollowness, like mushrooms from damp. Daily and nightly they alternate within us, but we cannot tell whence they spring. Can we then hope in a moment to lay our finger upon their very Cause?

But for these emotions I should not be. But for me, they would have no scope. So far we can go; but we do not know what it is that brings them into play. 'Twould seem to be a soul; but the clue to its existence is wanting. That such a Power operates, is credible enough, though we cannot see its form. It has functions without form.

—Chuang Tzŭ
Chuang Tzŭ, Mystic, Moralist, and Social Reformer.

The snow is fled: the trees their leaves put on,
The fields their green:
Earth owns the change, and rivers lessening run
Their banks between.
Naked the Nymphs and Graces in the meads
The dance essay:
"No 'scaping death" proclaims the year, that speeds
This sweet spring day.
Frosts yield to zephyrs; Summer drives out Spring,
To vanish, when
Rich Autumn sheds his fruits; round wheels the ring,
Winter again!

—Horace
"Odes 4.7." *The Odes and Carmen Saeculare of Horace.*

Times go by turns and chances change by course,
From foul to fair, from better hap to worse.

The sea of Fortune doth not ever flow,
She draws her favours to the lowest ebb;
Her tides hath equal times to come and go,
Her loom doth weave the fine and coarsest web;
No joy so great but runneth to an end,
No hap so hard but may in fine amend.
Not always fall of leaf nor ever spring,
No endless night yet not eternal day;
The saddest birds a season find to sing,
The roughest storm a calm may soon allay:
Thus with succeeding turns God tempereth all,
That man may hope to rise, yet fear to fall.

—ROBERT SOUTHWELL
"Times go by Turns." *The Oxford Book of English Verse: 1250–1900.*

From very low forms up to the highest—in the animal no less than in the vegetable kingdom—the process of life presents the same appearance of cyclical evolution. Nay, we have but to cast our eyes over the rest of the world and cyclical change presents itself on all sides. It meets us in the water that flows to the sea and returns to the springs; in the heavenly bodies that wax and wane, go and return to their places; in the inexorable sequence of the ages of man's life; in that successive rise, apogee, and fall of dynasties and of states which is the most prominent topic of civil history.

—THOMAS HENRY HUXLEY
"CCXXXIX". *Aphorisms and Reflections.*

The robin builds again in last year's tree,
And last year's stalk is blossoming this year's rose;
For Spring's young breast again the wild flower blows,
Back to the summer comes the loyal bee.

The moon returns unto the calling sea,
On waiting hills again the sunrise glows,
And, from the sweet land of the long ago's,
Imperishable memory comes to me.

—MARY ASHLEY TOWNSEND
"XXXIX." *Distaff and Spindle: Sonnets.*

In its largest sense, the principle of rhythm appears in all movements of nature and of life. It is heard and its effects are seen in all forms of wind and water, and less perceptibly in the solid forms of earth. There is no longer in books of science the idea of nature at rest. The throb of life is perpetual, and from the earth to language the rhythmic impulse prevails. It is the natural movement of energy.

—ORISON SWETT MARDEN
The Consolidated Library, Volume 8.

O BEAT and pause that count the life of man,
Throb of the pulsing heart!
Ripple of tides and stars beyond our scan!
Rhythm o' the ray o' the sun and the red o' the rose!
Thrill of the lightning's dart!
All, all are one beyond this world of shows.

Neither with eyes that see nor ears that hear
May we discern thee here,
Nor comprehend, O Life of life, thy laws,
But all our idols praise the perfect whole;
And I have worshipped thee, O rhythmic soul,
Chiefly in beat and pause.

O beat and pause that count the life of man,
Throb of the pulsing heart!
Ripple of tides and stars beyond our scan!
Rhythm o' the ray o' the sun and the red o' the rose!
Thrill of the lightning's dart!
Yea, all are one behind our world of shows.

—AGNES MARY FRANCES DUCLAUX
"Rhythm."

In all vibration is to be found a certain rhythm. Rhythm pervades the universe. The swing of the planets around the sun; the rise and fall of the sea; the beating of the heart; the ebb and flow of the tide; all follow rhythmic laws. The rays of the sun reach us; the rain descends upon us, in obedience to the same law. All growth is but an exhibition of this law. All motion is a manifestation of the law of rhythm.

—YOGI RAMACHARAKA
Hatha Yoga.

With beat of systole and of diastole
One grand great life throbs through earth's giant heart,
And mighty waves of single Being roll

From nerveless germ to man, for we are part
Of every rock and bird and beast and hill,
One with the things that prey on us, and one with what we kill....

We shall be
Parts of the mighty universal whole,
And through all aeons mix and mingle with the Kosmic Soul!

....

We shall be notes in that great Symphony
Whose cadence circles through the rhythmic spheres,
And all the live World's throbbing heart shall be
One with our heart; the stealthy creeping years
Have lost their terrors now, we shall not die,
The Universe itself shall be our Immortality!

—OSCAR WILDE
"Panthea." *Poems.*

Thus are all things seen to yearn
In due time for due return;
And no order fixed may stay,
Save which in th' appointed way
Joins the end to the beginning
In a steady cycle spinning.

—BOETHIUS
"Song II, Book III." *The Consolation of*
Philosophy of Boethius.

Chapter 12

The Law of Gender

The Law of Gender is declared to exist throughout nature and requires finding a balance between two opposing types of energy, masculine and feminine. In this sense of complementary opposites, this law is related to the Law of Polarity. The term "The Law of Gender", indicating masculine and feminine energies, has historical origins, although it is understood that these energies are not exclusively male or female, but can be present together in any individual or circumstance. The principle of duality embodied in this law has been described in other ways such as Yin and Yang of Taoist philosophy, and the interrelated opposites of introspective and extrospective character, and objective and subjective natures. The two types of energy are co-dependent and both are necessary for creative balance in our universe. This duality of energies is present in everything.

These qualities of Yin and Yang are complementary parts of a whole. The polar opposites of masculine and feminine energy, Yin and Yang, are necessary for creation in the tangible, physical word, and also in the intangible, non-physical world. Feminine energy is indicated in any growth or creative process, whether physical or non-physical in origin.

Masculine energy is considered to be the dynamic, active element that guides the conscious, objective part of our nature. Feminine energy is regarded as the passive, reflective element that guides the subjective, subconscious part of our nature. Both are desired and essential for balance in an individual's life, whether the individual is male or female.

In the non-physical dimension, the specific example of this law primarily refers to mental qualities, perspectives, and characteristics of the individual that are governed and balanced by conscience and a moral sense. The individual's objective is to find an equilibrium and balance between these two poles of energy in our character, behavior, and experiences.

"Gender is in everything; everything has its Masculine and Feminine Principles; Gender manifests on all planes."

—*The Kybalion*.

This Principle embodies the truth that there is GENDER manifested in everything—the Masculine and Feminine Principles ever at work. This is true not only of the Physical Plane, but of the Mental and even the Spiritual Planes.

No creation, physical, mental or spiritual, is possible without this Principle.

The Principle of Gender works ever in the direction of generation, regeneration, and creation.

—"The Seven Hermetic Principles."
The Kybalion.

First of all, there are the two opposite poles of masculine and feminine, which contain within them the entire of our humanity – which together, not separately, make up the whole of man.

—Frederick William Robertson
"Third Series. Sermon XV." *Sermons Preached at Brighton.*

The third requisite is endurance. "They bring forth fruit with patience." Patience is of two kinds. There is an active, and there is a passive endurance. the former is a masculine, the latter, for the most part, a feminine virtue.

—Frederick William Robertson
"First Series. Sermon II." *Sermons Preached at Brighton.*

Lastly, let me set before you, in one view, the incomparable excellencies and advantages of this lovely grace of Patience.

Patience is the guardian of faith, the preserver of peace, the cherisher of love, the teacher of humility. Patience governs the flesh, strengthens the spirit, stifles anger, extinguishes envy, subdues pride; she bridles the tongue, refrains the hand, tramples upon temptations, endures persecutions, consummates martyrdom. Patience produces unity in the church, loyalty in the state, harmony in families and societies; she comforts the poor and moderates the rich; she makes us humble in prosperity, cheerful in adversity, unmoved by calumny and reproach; she teaches us to forgive those who have injured us, and to be the first in asking forgiveness of those whom we have injured; she delights the faithful, and invites the unbelieving; she adorns the woman, and improves the man; is loved in a child, praised in a young man, admired in an old man; she is beautiful in either sex and every age.

—GEORGE HORNE (BISHOP OF NORWICH)
"Discourse X. Patience Portrayed." *Discourses on Several Subjects and Occasions.*

Thus closely following the male arts of use come the feminine arts of beauty,— painting, sculpture, architecture, music and poetry. " They weave and twine the heavenly roses in earthly life; they knit the bond of love which makes us blest, and in the chaste veil of the Graces, watchful, with holy hand, they cherish the eternal fire of delicate feelings."

—THEODORE PARKER
Lessons from the World of Matter and the World of Man.

The tendency of the Feminine Principle is always in the direction of receiving impressions, while the tendency of the Masculine Principle is always in the direction of giving, out or expressing. The Feminine Principle has much more varied field of operation than has the Masculine Principle. The Feminine Principle conducts the work of generating new thoughts, concepts, ideas, including the work of the imagination. The Masculine Principle contents itself with the work of the "Will" in its varied phases.

Persons who can give continued attention and thought to a subject actively employ both of the Mental Principles-the Feminine in the work of the mental generation, and the Masculine Will in stimulating and energizing the creative portion of the mind.

In fact, the Hermetic Teachings show that the very creation of the Universe follows the same law, and that in all creative manifestations, upon the planes of the spiritual, the mental, and the physical, there is always in operation this principle of Gender - this manifestation of the Masculine and the Feminine Principles.

—"Mental Gender." *The Kybalion.*

Contemplation generates; action propagates. Without the former, the latter is defective. Without the last, the first is abortive, and mere embryo. Saint Bernard compares contemplation to Rachael who was the most fair; but action to Leah, who was the most fruitful. I will neither always be busy and doing; nor ever be shut up in nothing but thoughts. Yet, that which some would call idleness, I will call the sweetest part of my life; and that is, meditation.

—Owen Felltham
Resolve, Divine, Moral and Political of Owen Felltham.

Myself am a little universe. Let my passions be moderate and my likes and dislikes be well-regulated, and then my conduct will conform of itself to the laws of the universe, in which the elements are so harmoniously combined. Heaven and earth are the great parents of all creation. If a man acts so as not to provoke the complaint of his fellow-creatures and not to bring disaster on all, he will become a spirit of universal fellowship and benevolence.

—Hung Ying-Ming
Musings of a Chinese Vegetarian.

The greatest power of mind, then, depends upon its exercise in moral channels, and therefore requires that every conscious mental effort should involve a moral end. A developed moral consciousness modifies consideration of motives, and increases the force and continuity of action; consequently the well developed symmetrical character necessitates good physical, mental and moral health, and this combination creates initiative, power, resistless force, and necessarily success.

—Charles F. Haanel
Mental Chemistry.

There is no town but has many sisters to every Lazarus, generous mothers, kindly aunts, faithful friends, whose footsteps are like those of spring, flowery to-day, in some weeks fruitful,— those who leave tracks of benevolence all through the cold and drifted snow of selfishness which piles the streets of a great metropolis. It is these persons, women and men, who carry on the great movements of mankind.

—Theodore Parker
Lessons from the World of Matter and the World of Man.

Duty is based upon a sense of justice—justice inspired by love, which is the most perfect form of goodness. Duty is not a sentiment, but a principle pervading the life: and it exhibits itself in conduct and in acts.

The voice of conscience speaks in duty done; and without its regulating and controlling influence, the brightest and greatest intellect may be merely as a light that leads astray.

Conscience is the moral governor of the heart—the governor of right action, of right thought, of right faith, of right life—and only through its dominating influence can the noble and upright character be fully developed.

—Samuel Smiles
"Chapter VII. Duty-Truthfulness." *Character.*

Do no violence to yourself, respect in yourself the oscillations of feeling. They are your life and your nature; One wiser than you ordained them. Do not abandon yourself altogether either to instinct or to will. Instinct is a siren, will a despot. Be neither the slave of your impulses and sensations of the moment, nor of an abstract and general plan; be open to what life brings from within and without, and welcome the unforeseen; but give to your life unity, and bring the unforeseen within the lines of your plan. Let what is natural in you raise itself to the level of the spiritual, and let the spiritual become once more natural. Thus will your development be harmonious....

—Henri-Frédéric Amiel
*Amiel's Journal: The Journal Intime
of Henri-Frédéric Amiel.*

Mind has a two-fold expression—conscious or objective, and subconscious or subjective. We come into relationship with the world without by the objective mind; and with the world within by the subconscious mind.

All Mind is One Mind; in all phases of the mental life there is an indivisible unity and oneness.

In the sub-consciousness is stored up the observations and experiences of life that have come to it through the conscious mind. It is the storehouse of memory. The subconscious mind is a great seed plot in which thoughts have been dropped, or experiences conveyed by observation, or happenings planted, to come up again into consciousness with the fruitage of their growth.

—Charles F. Haanel
Mental Chemistry.

When I dance, I dance; when I sleep, I sleep. Nay, when I walk alone in a beautiful orchard, if my thoughts are some part of the time taken up with external occurrences, I some part of the time call them back again to my walk, to the orchard, to the sweetness of that solitude, and to myself.

Nature has mother-like observed this, that the actions she has enjoined us for our necessity should be also pleasurable to us; and she invites us to them, not only by reason, but also by appetite, and 'tis injustice to infringe her laws. When I see alike Caesar and Alexander, in the midst of his greatest business, so fully enjoy human and corporal pleasures, I do not say that he relaxed his mind: I say that he strengthened it, by vigour of courage subjecting those violent employments and laborious thoughts to the ordinary usage of life: wise, had he believed the last was his ordinary, the first his extraordinary, vocation.

Relaxation and facility, methinks, wonderfully honour and best become a strong and generous soul.

Grandeur of soul consists not so much in mounting and in pressing forward, as in knowing how to govern and circumscribe itself; it takes everything for great, that is enough, and demonstrates itself better in moderate than in eminent things.

—Michel de Montaigne
"Chapter XIII. Of Experience. Book III."
The Essays of Michel de Montaigne.

To husband strength, mental and physical - to husband and govern power, passion, every impulse and every attribute of our nature, so that there may ever be with us the reserve-strength for use and enjoyment - is one of the chief secrets of happiness. Excess in pleasure or enjoyment is the bane of life. To stop a little short of the point of repletion is the golden secret.

—Prentice Mulford
"Coarse Gold."

Temperance, in the nobler sense, does not mean a subdued and imperfect energy; it does not mean a stopping short in any good thing, as in Love or in Faith; but it means the power which governs the most intense energy, and prevents its acting in any way but as it ought. And with respect to things in which there may be excess, it does not mean imperfect enjoyment of them; but the regulation of their quantity, so that the enjoyment of them shall be greatest.

—John Ruskin
"Early Renaissance." *Stones of Venice, Vol. 3.*

The spirit of emptiness is immortal.
It is called the Great Mother
because it gives birth to Heaven and Earth.

It is like a vapor,
barely seen but always present.
Use it effortlessly.

—Lao-Tzu
Tao Te Ching.

Giving birth and nourishing,
making without possessing,
expecting nothing in return.
To grow, yet not to control:
This is the mysterious virtue.

—Lao-Tzu
Tao Te Ching.

Temperance is reason's girdle and passion's bridle; the strength of the soul and the foundation of virtue.

—Jeremy Taylor
The Works of Jeremy Taylor D.D., Volume 1.

Nothing is good singly without its complement and its contrary. Self-examination is dangerous if it encroaches upon self-devotion; reverie is hurtful when it stupefies the will; gentleness is an evil when it lessens strength; contemplation is fatal when it destroys character. "Too much" and "too little" sin equally against wisdom. Excess is one evil, apathy another. Duty may be defined as energy tempered by moderation; happiness, as inclination calmed and tempered by self-control.

—Henri-Frédéric Amiel
Amiel's Journal. The Journal Intime of Henri-Frédéric Amiel.

There is a deep to which reason goes down with its flambeau in its hand; there is a height to which imagination goes up, on wide wings borne; and that is the deep of philosophy, that is the height of eloquence and song. But there is a deeper depth, where reason goes not, a higher height, where imagination never wanders; and that is the deep of justice, that is the height of love. It is the great wide heaven of religion. Conscience goes down there, affection goes up there, the soul lives up there. And that is the place of woman. Woman has gone deeper in justice, and has gone higher in love and trust, than man has gone.

—Theodore Parker
Lessons from the World of Matter and the World of Man.

The quality of mercy is not strained,
It droppeth as the gentle rain from heaven
Upon the place beneath. It is twice blest,
It blesseth him that gives and him that takes.
'Tis mightiest in the mightiest, it becomes
The thronèd monarch better than his crown.
His sceptre shows the force of temporal power,
The attribute to awe and majesty,
Wherein doth sit the dread and fear of kings;
But mercy is above this sceptred sway,
It is enthronèd in the hearts of kings,
It is an attribute to God himself,
And earthly power doth then show likest God's
When mercy seasons justice.

—WILLIAM SHAKESPEARE
"Act IV, Scene 1". *The Merchant of Venice.*

Generosity is a certain manly and womanly virtue, raised to a high power; meanness is an unmanly and unwomanly vice, carried down to the last degree. One is benevolence, felt with joy and achieved with alacrity; the other is selfishness cherished in the heart, rolled as a sweet morsel under the tongue, and applied in life to the fullest extent. Each may be regarded as an internal disposition,— that is, a mode of feeling, a form of character; and also as an outward manifestation,— a mode of action, a form of conduct.

Let us turn now to the more pleasing contemplation of generosity. What a beautiful excellence it is! Whether manifested in the pecuniary form of money, or of behavior, it is still the same thing,— justice mixed with love, leavened into beauty.

It is both a manly and a womanly virtue, so fair and sweet that it is always alike pleasant and profitable to dwell thereon...

For each example of meanness, I have a whole encyclopedia of generosity, a vast literature of generous men, and still more of generous women,— for this sweet violet of the heavenly spring, prophetic of a magnificent summer, like other tender and delicate virtues, thrives best in that fair warm soil on the feminine side of the human hill.

—Theodore Parker
Lessons from the World of Matter
and the World of Man.

Know the masculine,
but keep to the feminine:
and become a watershed to the world.
If you embrace the world,
the Tao will never leave you
and you become as a little child.

Know the white,
yet keep to the black:
be a model for the world.
If you are a model for the world,
the Tao inside you will strengthen
and you will return whole to your eternal beginning.

Know the honorable,
but do not shun the disgraced:
embracing the world as it is.
If you embrace the world with compassion,

then your virtue will return you to the uncarved block.

*The block of wood is carved into utensils
by carving void into the wood.
The Master uses the utensils, yet prefers to keep to the block
because of its limitless possibilities.
Great works do not involve discarding substance.*

—Lao-Tzu
Tao Te Ching.

*The Tao gave birth to One.
The One gave birth to Two.
The Two gave birth to Three.
The Three gave birth to all of creation.
All things carry Yin
yet embrace Yang.
They blend their life breaths
in order to produce harmony.*

—Lao-Tzu
Tao Te Ching.

Epilogue

THE UNIVERSAL LAWS

Before beginning, and without an end,
As space eternal and as surety sure,
Is fixed a Power divine which moves to good,
Only its laws endure.

This is its work upon the things ye see,
The unseen things are more; men's hearts and minds,
The thoughts of peoples and their ways and wills,
Those, too, the great Law binds.

—EDWIN ARNOLD
The Light of Asia: Or, The Great Renunciation.

The laws under which we live are designed solely for our advantage. These laws are immutable and we cannot escape from their operation. All the great eternal forces act in solemn silence, but it is within our power to place ourselves in harmony with them and thus express a life of comparative peace and happiness.

—CHARLES F. HAANEL
Mental Chemistry.

What are the sciences but maps of universal laws, and universal laws but the channels of universal power; and universal power but the outgoings of a universal mind? What are all physical phenomena properly understood, but the unfolding of a heart that delighteth to make the outgoings of the morning and evening to rejoice. .... All the forms and motions of matter are pervaded by wise design -

—Edward Thomson
"Spirituality." <i>Evidences of Revealed Religion.</i></div>

REFERENCES

Adler, Felix. *Life and Destiny: Or, Thoughts from the Ethical Lectures of Felix Adler.*

Allen, James. *Above Life's Turmoil.*

—-. *As A Man Thinketh.*

—-. *The Way of Peace.*

Allen, James Lane. *The Choir Invisible.*

Amiel, Henri-Frédéric. *Amiel's Journal: The Journal Intime of Henri-Frédéric Amiel.*

Arnold, Edwin. *The Light of Asia: Or, The Great Renunciation.*

Atkinson, William Walker. *Nuggets of the New Thought.*

—-. *Thought Vibration: Or, the Law of Attraction in the Thought World.*

Aurelius, Marcus. *The Meditations of Marcus Aurelius.* Translated by George Long.

Bacon, Francis. "Adversity." *Essays or Counsels Civil and Moral. The Works of Francis Bacon.*

Bailey, Philip James. *Festus, a Poem.*

Baron d'Holbach (Paul-Henri Thiry). *The System of Nature, Or, Laws of the Moral and Physical World.* Translated from the original, by Samuel Wilkinson, 1820-21.

Basford, James Lendall. *Sparks from the Philosopher's Stone.*

Bennett, Arnold. *How to Live on Twenty-four Hours a Day.*

Besant, Annie. *The Laws of the Higher Life.*

—-. *The Meaning and Method of the Spiritual Life.*

—-. *Some Problems of Life.*

The Bhagavad-Gita (From *The Mahabharata*). Translated from the Sanskrit Text by Sir Edwin Arnold.

Binney, Thomas. *Is it Possible to Make the Best of Both Worlds?*

Blake, William. "Auguries of Innocence."

Boethius. *The Consolation of Philosophy of Boethius.* Translated into English Prose and Verse by H. R. James.

Brhadaranyakopanishad. (The Spirit of the Upanishads; Or, The Aphorisms of the Wise.)

Brontë, Anne. "Views of Life." *Poems by Currer, Ellis, and Acton Bell.* (Charlotte Brontë, Emily Brontë and Anne Brontë).

Browning, Elizabeth Barrett. "An Essay on Mind." *An Essay on Mind, with Other Poems.*

—-. "Reward of Service."

Bryant, William Cullen. "To A Waterfowl."

Burroughs, John. *Accepting the Universe. Essays in Naturalism.*

—-. *Leaf and Tendril.*

—-. *Time and Change.*

Butler, Samuel. *The Way of All Flesh.*

Carlyle, Thomas. "Characteristics." *Critical and Miscellaneous Essays, Volume 5.*

—-. "Signs of the Time." *The Collected Works of Thomas Carlyle.*

Cary, Phoebe. "Now." *The Poetical Works of Alice and Phoebe Cary.*

Chapin, Edwin Hubbel. "Advice to the Young."

Chuang Tzu. *Chuang Tzu Mystic, Moralist, and Social Reformer.*

Clemmer, Mary. *Poems of Life and Nature.*

Coleridge, Samuel Taylor. "The Eolian Harp." *The Poems of Samuel Taylor Coleridge.*

Cowper, William. "The Task." *The Task and Other Poems.*

Cox, Kenyon. "Work Thou for Pleasure."

De Vere, Aubrey. "Sorrow."

The Dhammapada. Translated from the Pâli by F. Max Müller.

Dickens, Charles. *The Life and Adventures of Nicholas Nickleby.*

The Doctrine of the Mean. (Confucianism). Translated by James Legge.

Drummond, Henry. *Natural Law in the Spiritual World.*

Duclaux, Agnes Mary Frances. (Agnes Mary Frances Robinson). "Rhythm."

Dunbar, Paul Laurence. "The Lesson." *Lyrics of Lowly Life.*

Eliot, George (Mary Ann Evans). *Adam Bede.*

Emerson, Ralph Waldo. "The American Scholar."

—-. *The Divinity School Address.*

—-. *Essays, First Series.*

—-. *Essays, Second Series.*

—-. *Nature.*

—-. "Poetry and Imagination." *Letters and Social Aims. Volume 8.*

—-. "Success." *Society and Solitude.*

Epictetus. "VIII." *The Encheiridion, or Manual.* Translated by George Long.

Felltham, Owen. *Resolves, Divine, Moral and Political of Owen Felltham.* With some account of the author and his writings by James Cumming.

Fénelon, Francois de Salignac de La Mothe. *A Demonstration of the Existence and Attributes of God.*

—-. *Selections from Fénelon.*

Fichte, Johann Gottlieb. *The Destination of Man.* Translated from the German by Mrs. Percy Sinnett.

Fosdick, Harry Emerson. *Twelve Tests of Character.*

Fuller, Arthur Buckminster. "Preface." *Life Without and Life Within, Or, Reviews, Narratives, Essays, and Poems,* by Margaret Fuller.

Fuller, Margaret. *Life Without and Life Within, Or, Reviews, Narratives, Essays, and Poems.*

Gibran, Khalil. *The Prophet.*

Goethe, Johann Wolfgang von. *Faust.*

—-. *Goethe's Theory of Colours.* Translated from the German: with notes by Charles Lock Eastlake.

—-. *The Maxims and Reflections of Goethe.* Translated by Baily Saunders.

Gray, Thomas. "Ode on the Pleasure Arising from Vicissitude."

Grindon, Leo Hartley. *Life: Its Nature, Varieties, and Phenomena.*

Grou, Pere Jean Nicolas. *The Hidden Life of the Soul.*

Haanel, Charles F. *Mental Chemistry.*

Hartwig, Georg. *The Harmonies of Nature or The Unity of Creation.*

Hathaway, Benjamin. *Art-life And Other Poems.*

Hazlitt, William. "CCLXXXVII." *Characteristics: in the manner of Rochefoucault's Maxims.*

Henley, William Ernest. "Invictus."

Herbert, George. "Elixir."

Hill, Leslie Pinckney. "Compensation." *The Wings of Oppression.*

Hill, Napoleon. *Think and Grow Rich.*

Horace (Quintus Horatius Flaccus). *The Odes and Carmen Saeculare of Horace.*

Horton, George Moses. "Departing Summer."

Horne, George. (Bishop of Norwich). *Discourses on Several Subjects and Occasions.*

Hume, David. *An Enquiry Concerning the Human Understanding, And An Enquiry Concerning the Principles of Morals.*

—-. *Essays Moral, Political, and Literary.*

Hung Ying-Ming. *Musings of a Chinese Vegetarian.* Translated by Yaichiro Isobe.

Huxley, Thomas Henry. *Aphorisms and Reflections.* Selected by Henrietta A. Huxley.

Ingersoll, Robert Green. "Nature." *The Philosophy of Ingersoll.* Edited and arranged by Vere Goldthwaite.

James, William. *The Varieties of Religious Experience.*

Jefferies, Richard. *The Pageant of Summer.*

Johnson, Samuel. *The Adventurer. (The Works of Samuel Johnson), LL.D., in Nine Volumes, Volume the Second.*

—-. T*he Rambler. Vol. 1.*

Jordan, William George. *The Majesty of Calmness.*

The Kybalion. By the Three Initiates (often identified as William Walker Atkinson).

Lao-Tzu. *Tao Te Ching.* A translation for the public domain by J. H. McDonald.

Longfellow, Henry Wadsworth. *Kavanagh, A Tale.*

—-. *Keramos and Other Poems.*

—-. "A Psalm of Life."

—-. "Sunrise on the Hills."

—-. "The Wind Over the Chimney."

Lowell, James Russell. *Poems of James Russell Lowell.*

Lubbock, John. *The Pleasures of Life: Part II.*

"Majjhima-Nikaya ii.32". *The Middle-length Discourses of the Buddha.*

Malloch, Douglas. "Sympathy." *In Forest Land.*

Manning, Henry Edward. *Sermons, Volume the Fourth.*

Marden, Orison Swett. *The Consolidated Library, Volume 8.*

—-. *The Consolidated Library, Volume 14.*

Markham, Edwin. "Two at a Fireside." *The Man with the Hoe, and Other Poems.*

Martineau, Harriet. "Preface." *The Positive Philosophy of Auguste Comte.* (Freely translated by Harriet Martineau).

Martineau, James. *Endeavours After the Christian Life.*

McKay, Charles. "Serenity." *Voices from the Mountains and from the Crowd.*

Meynell, Alice. "The Rhythm of Life." *The Rhythm of Life And Other Essays.*

Montaigne, Michel de. *The Essays of Michel de Montaigne.* Translated by Charles Cotton. Edited by William Carew Hazlitt.

Morgan, Angela. "Reality." *Utterance And Other Poems.*

Morris, Lewis. *The Ode of Life.*

Mountford, William. *Thorpe: A Quiet English Town, and Human Life Therein.*

Mulford, Prentice. "Coarse Gold."

—-. *Your Forces, and How to Use Them, Volume 1.*

Naidu, Sarojini. "The Soul's Prayer." *The Bird of Time. Songs of Life, Death & the Spring.*

Norris, Alfred. "A Prayer." *Inner and Outer Life: Poems.*

Novalis (Georg Philipp Friedrich Freiherr von Hardenberg). *From Forty Thousand Sublime and Beautiful Thoughts.* Compiled by Charles Noel Douglas.

Noyes, Alfred. "The Loom of Years." *Collected Poems, Volume 1.*

Osgood, Frances S. "Music." *The Female Poets of America.*

Osler, William. *A Way of Life (An Address to Yale Students Sunday Evening, April 20th, 1913).*

Ovid (Publius Ovidius Naso) *Metamorphoses, XV.* Translated by Sir Samuel Garth, John Dryden, et. al.

Panchadasi. (The Spirit of the Upanishads; Or, The Aphorisms of the Wise.)

Parker, Theodore. *Lessons from the World of Matter and the World of Man.*

Pascal, Blaise. *Pensées (Thoughts.)* Translated by William Finlayson Trotter.

Phelps, Egbert. "Life's Incongruities."

Plutarch. "On Contentedness of Mind." *Plutarch's Morals: Ethical Essays.*

Pope, Alexander. *An Essay on Man. Moral Essays and Satires.*

Popular Science Monthly. Volume 3, May 1873.

Prince, John Critchley. *Hours with the Muses.*

Prior, Matthew. *Solomon on the Vanity of the World. A Poem. In Three Books*

Procter, Adelaide Anne. "Give." *Legends and Lyrics: A Book of Verses.*

Procter, Bryan Waller. (pseud. Barry Cornwall). "The Gauge of Life."

Richter, Jean Paul Friedrich. *Hesperus or Forty-Five Dog-Post-Days Vol. I. A Biography.* Translated by Charles T. Brooks.

Robertson, Frederick William. *Sermons Preached at Brighton.*

Ruskin, John. *The Seven Lamps of Architecture.*

—-. *Stones of Venice, Vol. 2 & 3.*

—-. *The Works of John Ruskin.*

S'ankaracharya. *The Spirit of the Upanishads; Or, The Aphorisms of the Wise.*

Scott, Sir Walter. *Marmion.*

Seneca, Lucius Annaeus. "Of a Happy Life."

Shabistari, Mahmud. *The Secret Rose Garden of Sa'd Ud Din Mahmud Shabistari.*

Shairp, John Campbell. *On Poetic Interpretation of Nature.*

Shakespeare, William. *Hamlet.*

—-. *The Merchant of Venice.*

Shelley, Percy Bysshe. "Mutability."

Shinn, Florence Scovel. *The Game of Life and How to Play It.*

Smiles, Samuel. *Character.*

Southwell, Robert. "Times go by Turns." *The Oxford Book of English Verse: 1250–1900.*

Spinoza, Benedict de. *The Ethics (Ethica Ordine Geometrico Demonstrata).* Translated by R. H. M. Elwes.

Street, Alfred Billings. "Nature." *The Poems of Alfred B. Street.*

Swami Vivekananda (born Narendranath Datta*). The Complete Works of Swami Vivekananda.*

Tao Te Ching by Lao-Tzu, Complete online text, a translation for the public domain by J. H. McDonald. 1996.

Taylor, Jeremy. *The Works of Jeremy Taylor D.D., Volume 1.*

Thomson, Edward. *Evidences of Revealed Religion.*

Thoreau, Henry David. *Walden.*

—-. *The Writings of Henry David Thoreau.*

Three Initiates (often identified as William Walker Atkinson). *The Kybalion.*

Tilton, Theodore. "The Chant Celestial." *Thou and I: a lyric of human life. With other poems.*

—-. "The Mystery of Nature." *The Sexton's Tale, and Other Poems.*

Townsend, Mary Ashley. *Distaff and Spindle: Sonnets.*

Traherne, Thomas. *Centuries of Meditations.*

Trench, Richard Chenevix. *Sabbation; Honor Neale; and Other Poems.*

Trine, Ralph Waldo. *Character-Building Thought Power.*

—-. *In Tune with the Infinite.*

Trowbridge, John Townsend. "Twoscore and Ten." *A Home Idyl: And Other Poems.*

Tupper, Martin Farquhar. *Proverbial Philosophy: A Book of Thoughts and Arguments.*

Van Dyke, Henry. "Thoughts Are Things."

Vivekachudamani. (*The Spirit of the Upanishads; Or, The Aphorisms of the Wise.*)

Wagner, Charles. *The Better Way.*

Whewell, William. "Treatise III." *The Bridgewater Treatises.*

Whitman, Albery Allson. *The Rape of Florida.*

Whitman, Walt. "Song of Joys." *Leaves of Grass.*

Wilcox, Ella Wheeler. *Poems of Passion.*

—-. *Poems of Power.*

—-. *Poems of Optimism.*

Wilde, Oscar. "Panthea." *Poems.*

Wordsworth, William." *Lyrical Ballads, with a Few Other Poems.*

Yogavasishtha. (*The Spirit of the Upanishads; Or, The Aphorisms of the Wise.*)

Yogi Ramacharaka. *Hatha Yoga or the Yogi Philosophy of Physical Well-being.*

Young, Edward. "Night Sixth." *Night Thoughts, on Life, Death, and Immortality.*

www.ingramcontent.com/pod-product-compliance
Lightning Source LLC
LaVergne TN
LVHW010204070526
838199LV00062B/4499